Istanbul

G000135442

An architectural guide

•••

Christa Beck and Christiane Forsting

Istanbul

An architectural guide

••• **ellipsis** KÖNEMANN

• • •

CREATED, EDITED AND DESIGNED BY
Ellipsis London Limited
55 Charlotte Road London EC2A 3QT
E MAIL ...@ellipsis.co.uk
WWW http://www.ellipsis.co.uk/ellipsis
PUBLISHED IN THE UK AND AFRICA BY
Ellipsis London Limited
SERIES EDITOR Tom Neville
EDITOR Vicky Wilson
SERIES DESIGN Jonathan Moberly
LAYOUT Pauline Harrison

COPYRIGHT © 1997 Könemann
Verlagsgesellschaft mbH
Bonner Str. 126, D-50968 Köln
PRODUCTION MANAGER Detlev Schaper
PRINTING AND BINDING Sing Cheong
Printing Ltd
Printed in Hong Kong

ISBN 3 89508 638 X (Könemann)
ISBN 1 899858 31 8 (Ellipsis)

Christa Beck and Christiane Forsting 1997

Contents

Introduction

Though the buildings of Istanbul's Byzantine and Ottoman eras have been well documented, little has been written about the heritage of the nineteenth century and next to nothing about the city's contemporary architecture. This guide therefore focuses on the architecture of the nineteenth and twentieth centuries, while including key historic buildings that have stood the test of time, help with an understanding of the context of more recent architecture, and in many cases contain revelations for twentieth-century eyes.

The only city to stand on two continents – Europe and Asia – Istanbul is divided by the Bosphorus strait, which flows from the Black Sea to the Sea of Marmara. The seven hills of the peninsula of Stamboul (probably a corruption of the Greek *stin polin* meaning 'in the city'), the oldest section of the city containing the majority of its historic monuments, are bounded by the waters of the Golden Horn (Haliç) to the north, the Sea of Marmara to the south and the Bosphorus to the east. Of the areas covered in this book, the port area of Galata in the district of Beyoğlu, the districts of Beşiktaş and Şişli, and the area we refer to as 'Bosphorus European side' lie on the other side of the Golden Horn. On the Asian side of the Bosphorus are Üsküdar and Kadıköy to the south, opposite Stamboul, with the 'Bosphorus Asian side' area to the north and the summer resort of the Princes' Isles some 15 to 30 kilometres south along the Marmara coast.

Archaeological evidence indicates that there was a settlement in the area of the Bosphorus strait and Golden Horn as early as 2000 BC, but little is known about the history of what was to become Constantinople and then Istanbul until the founding of Byzantium, one of the richest colonial cities of ancient Greece, in the seventh century BC. Sited on Stamboul's first hill, Byzantium lay on the caravan trading route – the silk road – between China and the Mediterranean and was in a position to control the shipping between the Black Sea and Sea of Marmara. From 512 BC, when it was conquered by Darius of Persia, until the second century BC, the city oscillated between Persian, Athenian, Spartan and Macedonian rule. In AD 73 it became part of the Roman province of Asia.

THE BYZANTINE EMPIRE

In AD 324 Constantine, Roman emperor of the west, defeated Licinius, Roman emperor of the east, in a battle near Byzantium to become sole emperor of Rome. He moved the capital to Byzantium, which became known as Constantinople ('city of Constantine'). He swiftly rebuilt the city to suit its new role, quadrupling its size and introducing straight wide streets and impressive monuments such as the column of Constantine and its surrounding forum. The building programme, begun in 326, took less than four years to complete and on 11 May 330 Constantine dedicated the city as capital of his empire. His monumental work was continued by subsequent emperors such as Valens (364–78), who constructed a water-supply system to the inner city that includes the aqueduct of Valens.

Constantine took on the role of head of the church as well as of the state, espousing Christianity, though Christians were still a minority in his empire. Theodosius I (379–95) established Christianity as the state religion soon after his accession to the throne; after his death the empire once more split into two: the western part, with its Roman Catholic faith, was governed from Rome and the eastern part, with its Greek Orthodox faith, from Byzantium.

By the time of Theodosius II (408–50) the city had expanded to such an extent that a new city wall was needed, the Theodosian land wall. At this time the Galata area was also developed, acquiring churches, theatres, baths and a harbour.

The heyday of the Byzantine empire was in the reign of Justinian I (527–65), who extended it to cover an area almost the size of the Roman empire under Augustus. Justinian survived a major revolt in 532 during which most of the buildings on the first hill were destroyed. He embarked on a massive programme of reconstruction, building on an even more monumental scale than before. The jewel in the crown was the rebuilt Haghia Sophia, a symbol of power and expression of the modern Christian era and a monument that surpassed all others in scale and construction. The Yerbatan Sarayı cistern also dates from Justinian's reign.

The empire continued to be threatened by the Persians, Arabs, Bulgars and others, though from the accession of Heracleonas in 610 to the death of Basil II in 1025 – the heroic age – it was ruled by a series of great warrior emperors. The city of Constantinople became increasingly independent of its Roman model and Greek was established as the official language. But the empire was also beset by internal disputes, including that between the Iconoclasts, who supported Leo III's edict of 730 ordering the destruction of all figurative religious representations in homes and churches, and the Iconodules, who wanted sacred images restored. The crisis was not resolved until 843, when a synod of the Greek Orthodox church in the Haghia Sophia opted for the restoration of icons. In the meantime, however, irreparable damage had been sustained.

For a century from 1081 the empire was ruled by the Comnenus dynasty (see church of the Pantocrator). An agreement with Venice allowing tax-free trade led to an influx of foreigners, and by the middle of the twelfth century over 60,000 were living in Constantinople. The death of Manuel I – the last great Byzantine emperor – in 1180 was followed by a series of rebellions and depositions that culminated in the sacking of the city in 1204 by crusaders called in to support the claims to the throne of the deposed Isaac II. The city was divided up, with almost half its land, including the church of Haghia Sophia, going to the Venetians. But Latin Constantinople ('Latin' was the term used to describe western Christians) was weak, and fragments of the former Byzantine empire outside the city continued to be ruled by various members of former royal families, strongest of which was the empire of Nicea. In 1261 Michael VII Palaeologus of Nicea made a triumphal entry into Constantinople, establishing the last of the Byzantine empire's great dynasties.

Apart from the Theodosian land wall, elements of the water-supply network and a few scattered monuments, the major survivors of the Byzantine empire are its churches. In the early Byzantine period most churches were basilicas – typically rectangular buildings divided along the long axis by two rows of columns into a central nave flanked by two aisles. The semi-circular apse is at the eastern end and the entrance, with an inner and sometimes an outer vestibule leading to an arcaded courtyard, at the western end. Early basilicas had pitched roofs and flat ceilings but later domes were introduced.

In the second half of the ninth century, as a spate of new church building began in the wake of the settling of the Iconoclast crisis, a new form, the cross-domed church, was developed. Here a central dome is surrounded on the axes of the building by four long barrel vaults resting on corner piers to form a cruciform plan. At the eastern end is a wide central apse flanked by two smaller apses and at the western end an interior vestibule. A variation on this plan is the four-column church (see church of the Pantocrator), where four columns take the place of the piers. Small (in line with the empire's declining fortunes), tall and almost square from the outside, these churches retained the cruciform plan within, leaving copious space for decoration. All Constantinople's Byzantine churches were built of brick, with relatively sober exteriors but extravagantly decorated interiors using marble for the lower walls and predominantly gold mosaics for upper walls, vaults and domes.

THE OTTOMAN EMPIRE

The rise of the Osmanlı Turks or Ottomans in Asia Minor began in the thirteenth century under Osman I (1288–1326). In 1326 his son Orhan (1326–60) captured the Byzantine city of Brusa (now Bursa) near the Sea of Marmara, which he transformed into his capital. The Ottomans soon conquered most of western Asia Minor and advanced into Europe as far as the Danube. In 1365 Murat I made Edirne (Adrianople) their capital, expressing their interest in the European part of the empire.

Mehmet II succeeded to the throne in 1451, aged 19, and immediately made preparations for the siege of Constantinople. In 1451–2 he built the Rumeli fortress on the European side of the Bosphorus opposite the Anadolu fortress of 1394 on the Asian side, enabling him to blockade the strait, cutting the city off from the Black Sea and its grain supplies. The siege began in March 1453 and lasted seven weeks. On the morning of 29 May the sultan's all-out attack was finally successful. In the afternoon he rode in triumph to Haghia Sophia, which he ordered to be converted into a mosque, and the following Friday attended the first Muslim service there.

Mehmet Fatih (Conqueror) soon began rebuilding the city. He built his first palace to the north of what is now Beyazıt Square, today the site of the university, and in 1465 began the Topkapı Sarayı, residence of the Ottoman sultans until the nineteenth century. He completed the great

Fatih Camii (mosque of the Conqueror) in 1470 and in the course of his reign a further 190 new mosques were built and 18 former churches converted, many the centre of a complex of pious foundations and religious and philanthropic institutions called a *külliye*. A decree valid until the nineteenth century forbade the presence of non-Muslim buildings on the city's skyline, contributing greatly to Istanbul's acquisition and maintenance of an Islamic character, though a spirit of tolerance allowed Greeks, Armenians and Jews full rights. Mehmet also established the city's first covered bazaar, the Kapalı Çarşısı, on its present site, and repopulated the city, which had lost many of its inhabitants in the decades before the conquest.

While axial streets and squares were a feature of Roman urban planning, Ottoman urban principles demanded that architecture respond to topography. The most important buildings, the mosques, were sited on hilltops, and little attention was paid to the streets below. As a built expression of the Islamic belief that everything earthly is temporary, holy buildings – the mosques and their *külliye* – were monumental in scale and built in stone, while most other structures, including the pavilions that made up the royal palaces, were small in scale and usually of timber construction.

Mehmet's son Beyazit II (1481–1512) greatly developed the empire's trade and commerce, while his son and successor Selim I expanded its boundaries, adding Egypt in 1517. He was succeeded by Süleyman the Magnificent (1520–66), who expanded the empire as far as Vienna and Algiers. Loot from his many campaigns was used to embellish Istanbul with palaces and mosques, most famous of which is the Süleymaniye mosque, the work of the architect Sinan.

In his 50 years as chief of the imperial architects (1538–88) Sinan

Istanbul: an architectural guide

contributed some 40 large mosques to the city and established a typology that remained largely unchallenged until the eighteenth century. As with the Süleymaniye, the mosques of the classical period derive from a fusion of native Ottoman tradition with elements from the plan of the Haghia Sophia, removing as many of the basilica's columns as possible to make the interior more open and transparent. Most of the large imperial mosques have a central dome supported by two semidomes of equal diameter to the east and west; in some cases (see the Sultan Ahmet I mosque) two more semidomes are added at the south and north to increase the open space and centralisation of the plan. Most mosques have a porch leading into a monumental courtyard surrounded on three sides by a domed arcade with a *şadırvan* (central fountain for ritual ablutions) and an impressive gateway opposite the mosque's main entrance. Small mosques have a single minaret, the imperial mosques usually have two or four, and the Sultan Ahmet I mosque boasts six. The most important element in the interior is the *mihrab*, a niche in the centre of the wall opposite the main entrance that indicates the direction of Mecca. The imperial mosques have a royal lodge, sometimes accessible from the outside, screened off from the rest of the interior by a grille.

Most of the imperial mosques are attached to a *külliye*, usually arranged around four sides of a central arcaded courtyard and consisting of a combination of some or all of the following elements: a *medrese* (religious school), *daruşşifa* (hospital), *tımarhane* (insane asylum), *kervansaray* offering accommodation and meals to travellers and *imaret* (public kitchen). The founder usually built his *türbe* or mausoleum in the mosque garden or graveyard.

Other important public institutions dating from the Ottoman period include the *han*, originally the same as a *kervansaray* but often with attached workshops and storage space for traders' wares, the *hamam* or baths, the covered bazaars, and the *çeşme* or fountain. Istanbul today retains more than 700 fountains dating from the Ottoman era. They range from grandiose imperial street fountains through less elaborate *sebils* or fountain houses – freestanding domed structures with grilled façades from which an attendant would serve travellers with cups of water – to niches furnished with a water spout and marble basin.

While the traditional Turkish house would adapt its form to the demands of the site, the freestanding houses of the elite, mostly timber framed, developed a symmetrical plan based around a central area, the *sofa* or hallway, giving access to the other spaces – a plan dating back to the fifteenth-century Çinili Köşkü. Typical elements include overhanging eaves, vertical window elements, bay windows which make rectangular rooms and views outside possible on the upper floors, even if the ground floor adapts to an irregular site, and grilles which allow views out but prevent those inside from being seen – important since Islam forbade women to appear in public without a veil. Men and women occupied separate sets of rooms – the women the *harem* and the men the *selamlık*. The city was subject to a series of earthquakes and fires – between 1633 and 1906 there were 229 extensive fires in Stamboul and Galata. The Aksaray fire of 1856 and Hocapaşa fire of 1865 in particular played a major part in reshaping Stamboul.

Muslims were allowed four wives and as many concubines as they wished. The imperial *harem* was ruled by the sultan's mother, the valide sultan, and his chief wife, the first kadın. Süleyman's first kadın was a woman he called Haseki Hürrem (the Joyous Favourite), known in the west as Roxelana. Roxelana's power was immense, allowing her to order the elimination of the Grand Vezir Ibrahim Paşa and to insist on the succession going to her own son Selim the Sot (Selim II), whose reign marked the start of the empire's long decline. For the next century a series of strong women took control of the affairs of the palace from their weak sons or husbands.

The beginning of the nineteenth century saw a movement for reform (*Tanzimat*) influenced by developments in western Europe, including the French revolution. Between 1826 and 1876 sultans Mahmut II, Abdül Mecit and Abdül Aziz initiated a series of constitutional measures that culminated in the establishment of a parliament in 1877. But this period of democracy was shortlived and the following year the new sultan Abdül Hamit II dissolved parliament, revoked the constitution and began three decades of despotic rule.

In the second half of the eighteenth century Istanbul had had its first contact with European architectural fashions, beginning with the introduction of the Ottoman baroque, as in the Nuruosmaniye mosque of 1748–55, the first significant building to display the new baroque style. The nineteenth century saw the increased westernisation and modernisation of the capital. The arrival of the ferries, horse-drawn trams and railway required the introduction of new building types (see the Sirkeci and Haydarpaşa stations and Beşiktaş landing stage), as well as leading to increasing mobility and opening up the Asian shore to settlement. Architecturally, eclecticism prevailed, with neo-classicism the dominant style. European and European-trained architects were favoured over those with a Turkish architectural education, the most influential architectural dynasty being the Balyan family, architects of the monumental European-style Dolmabahçe and Çırağan palaces.

During this period France and Germany vied for economic and cultural dominance in Istanbul. The School of Fine Arts (now the Mimar Sinan

University), modelled on the Parisian Ecole des Beaux-Arts, was opened in 1882 and the German-influenced School of Civil Engineering (now the Istanbul Technical University) two years later. Among the European architects working in Istanbul were the Frenchman Alexandre Vallaury (see Istanbul High School), who taught at the School of Fine Arts and was chief of the imperial architects and the German Jachmund (see Sirkeci station and German Oriental Bank), who had been given a grant from the German government to study Ottoman architecture and taught at the School of Civil Engineering.

Art nouveau was introduced by the Italian Raimondo D'Aronco (see Laleli fountain) who lived in Istanbul from 1893 to 1909 and was chief of the imperial architects from 1896 to 1908. The area in which the westernisation of the city is most apparent is Beyoğlu, which became popular with rich merchants and foreign ambassadors in the nineteenth century, leading to the introduction of impressive European-style mansions with large gardens, European-style hotels and department stores and shopping arcades. The architectural fashions of Istanbul can be traced through the *yalı*s (mansions on the shores of the Bosphorus, see Bosphorus mansions) which in the course of the nineteenth century moved from baroque to empire to eclectic cosmopolitan style.

Sultan Abdül Hamit II was deposed in 1909 by the Young Turks, an alliance of military and intellectuals whose nationalistic wing set up a military dictatorship under the leadership of Enver Bey and Talat Bey, who in 1914 brought Turkey into the First World War on the side of Germany. In August 1919 Sultan Mehmet VI was forced by the Allies to sign the Treaty of Sèvres, which stripped the empire of all its territory except Istanbul and that part of Anatolia not under Allied occupation. But many people rejected the solution, joining the nationalist movement and war of liberation led by Mustafa Kemal Paşa (later Atatürk). Following the defeat of the Greek army and the signature of the Treaty of Lausanne, which established the boundaries of modern Turkey, the Turkish National Assembly declared the founding of the Turkish Republic with Atatürk as its first president on 29 October 1923. Religion and state policy were separated, the capital was moved to Ankara, and for the first time for 1600 years Istanbul lost its position as a capital.

THE TURKISH REPUBLIC

The establishment of Ankara as the new capital led to a spate of building activity in Turkey as the embassies and other political institutions gradually moved their headquarters to the new political centre. The favoured architectural style from the First Balkan War (1912) was the first national architectural movement, pioneered by Kemalettin Bey (see Hotel Merit Antique) and Vedat Tek (see Central Post Office), in which architects combined elements of their Ottoman heritage and of international eclecticism with contemporary western building technology to create a national architecture appropriate to but not slavishly imitative of its surroundings. Typically Ottoman elements such as pointed arches, bay windows and overhanging eaves would be amalgamated with steel or reinforced-concrete construction. The first national architectural movement was largely replaced by modernism from 1929 until the outbreak of the Second World War, fuelled by the need to create Ankara as the new capital, influenced by the number of foreign architects working there and justified by the economic depression which made unneccessary ornament seem wasteful. Though Ankara embraced a pure form of modernism, much international-style-influenced architecture in Istanbul remained eclectic (see Mehmet Efendi coffee shop).

A reaction against modernism – influenced by the rise in nationalist architecture elsewhere in Europe, particularly in Germany, and the shortage of steel, glass and cement brought about by the Second World War – led to the development of the second national architectural movement (1940–50) headed by Sedad Hakkı Eldem (see Şark restaurant), one of the most influential architects in contemporary Turkey who taught at the School of Fine Arts and was responsible for more than 100 buildings in a 50-year-long career. Eldem was influenced by German architects Paul Bonatz, an architectural advisor to the Turkish government and professor at the School of Civil Engineering, and Clemens Holzmeister and Bruno Taut, all of whom contributed important buildings to Ankara in the 1930s and 1940s. Unlike the first national architectural movement, which was an effort to retrieve the lost glory of Ottoman architecture, the second national architectural movement refuses formal imitation. Its debt to tradition resides in the overall character of the building – the abundance of windows, the plan types, the materials and methods of construction: using native craftsmen and concealing modern materials. These buildings of the war years reflect an atmosphere of nationalism and resistance to external pressures. Both national movements were retreats to historical forms in times of national crisis.

The end of the war saw the return of the international style (see Istanbul City Hall), though during the 1960s some architects, including Eldem, embraced a form of new regionalism (see Social Security Agency complex). High-tech architecture has made little impact, and to judge by the results of recent architectural competitions, post-modernism seems to be the style of the moment. But the buildings that make up most of the new urban fabric – the self-built *gecekondu* (literally 'built overnight') housing and typical housing blocks – have bypassed architects altogether.

Istanbul: an architectural guide

The first mass *gecekondu* developments began at the end of the Second World War and the phenomenon continues today. This self-help building movement arose as the result of the massive rural exodus spurred by the 'tractor years' (the mechanisation of Turkey's agriculture) and the need for labour in the cities. Migrants settled near industrial areas on the outskirts, where unregulated building activity on public or agricultural land was easier. In Istanbul, early *gecekondu*s include that at Zeytinburnu, on the outskirts, as well as smaller ones in Beyoğlu, Mecidiyeköy, the run-down areas of Stamboul, Üsküdar and around some of the Bosphorus villages.

The attitude of the government was ambivalent: on the one hand, this self-built housing reduced shortages without requiring public spending, but on the other, the uncontrolled growth meant that local authorities could not provide any basic infrastructure, resulting in social, economic and ecological disasters. *Gecekondu* amnesty laws, which gave inhabitants right of possesion, were followed by measures to prevent further construction through state investment in cheap housing and the elimination of existing settlements.

Over the years, the amnesty laws have led in some cases to the gradual transformation of *gecekondu* settlements into conventional urban districts, as at Zeytinburnu. But at the same time, new *gecekondu*s have continued to be built, making urban planning impossible and exhausting the city's natural resources. In Istanbul in 1975 approximately 50 per cent of the inhabitants lived in *gecekondu*s. From the 1980s temporary settlements have been built illegally by 'contractors' who sell or rent to impoverished people – a kind of mafia infrastructure. The meaning of *gecekondu* today is 'illegal development'.

The other typical housing is faceless blocks of flats – speculative

schemes providing accommodation for middle-income families which
have often required the demolition of historic areas. Planning regulations
demand that the blocks are freestanding, ensuring that no urban spaces
are created, while the need for many circulation streets reduces the potential for green space. Such settlements are popular because of the quality
of their infrastructure: unlimited water and electricity, paved roads and
street lighting are usually supplied. Most of the blocks built in the last
three decades consist of freehold flats, generous in size and with good
natural lighting. They have concrete frames, stiffened with brick walls
to resist modest earthquakes, but no insulation and a low standard of
workmanship.

Istanbul has always been a cultural melting pot and it is the resolution
of differences and opposites that gives it its unique character. The city is
both Asian and European. In the old city centre money changes hands
in streets filled with people and traffic; in the antiseptic new business areas
all transactions take place electronically.

The outlook is bleak. Uncontrolled building speculation and lack of
an efficient enforcement of planning regulations are destroying histori-
cally important areas; the population explosion and concomitant traffic
chaos are overburdening the infrastructure. The city's picturesque skyline
is being lost and its relation to the water has been eroded by the construction of the coastal roads and bridges that have deprived the waterfront
of its quality as a lively urban space. Building basic accommodation for
the influx of settlers takes up most of the city's resources with nothing
left for luxury or monuments. The necessity of maximising the financial
return from commercial buildings and high-rent housing leaves little
space for the rediscovery of an architectural culture.

But steps are being taken to improve the situation. Gas pipes are being laid to reduce the pollution from coal-burning fires; a metro is being built; the polluted Golden Horn is being cleaned up; historic buildings are being restored. Architects like Nevzat Sayın strive to find new ways of reducing building costs without a reduction in architectural quality; planners work with new urban solutions to create new urban spaces. The chamber of architects is actively engaged in rescuing the city's heritage and there is a growing concern among building professionals to reduce energy consumption by providing improved insulation.

Istanbul has its share of individuals who try to swim against the tide and build meaningful architecture alongside the mass of building activity. It is to be hoped that their combined efforts will halt the destruction of the city's heritage and create a contemporary contribution of which future generations can be proud.

ACKNOWLEDGEMENTS
Thanks to our friends Mark Asipowicz and Yaşar Öncü for help with English and Turkish respectively, for accompanying us to several sites, for discussing architecture and for helping with photographs; to Şeref Aynacıoğlu for help with computers; to Arif Çağlar for organising appointments and helpful tips; to architects and friends in Istanbul, especially İhsan Bilgin and Mr and Mrs Said Kuran, who made the book possible and made our stay a very special experience; to our friends and family who encouraged us to write this book; and to our publisher Tom Neville.

The photographs of the Sabah newspaper works, Brav boutique, Shell general headquarters and Hasol mansion were supplied by the architects; those of Sadullah Paşa Yalısı are by Cemal Emden; that of the interior of the Süleymaniye mosque is by Charles Neale.

Bibliography

Akçura, G, *The Golden Horn of Istanbul*, Istanbul 1992
Arın, C, *Ausländer im Wohnbereich*, Berlin 1983
Arredamento Dekorasyon Magazins, Istanbul
Belge, M, *İstanbul Gezi Rehberi*, Istanbul 1993
Bruttomesso, R, *Waterfronts: a new frontier for cities on water*, Venice 1993
Çelik, Z, *The Remaking of Istanbul*, Seattle and London 1986
Dökmeci, V & Çıracı, H, *Beyoğlu, Tarihsel Gelişim Sürecinde*, Istanbul 1990
Eldem, S H, *Boğaziçi Anıları*, Istanbul 1979
Eldem, S H, *İstanbul Anıları*, Istanbul 1979
Ertuğ, A & Quigley-Pınar, M, *Istanbul: gateway to splendour*, Istanbul 1986
Freely, J, *Blue Guide Istanbul*, London 1991
Freely, J, *The Bosphorus*, Istanbul 1993
Goodwin, G A, *History of Ottoman Architecture*, London 1971
Hellier C, *Villen und Paläste am Bosphorus*, London 1993
Holod R & Evin A, *Modern Turkish Architecture*, Pennsylvania 1984
Institut Français d'Architecture, Mimar, *Architecture in development – Istanbul*, Paris 1987
İstanbul Dergiler, Istanbul
Küçükerman, Ö, *Das alttürkische Wohnhaus*, Istanbul 1978
Kültür Bakanlığı ve Tarih Vakfının Ortak Yayınıdır, *İstanbul Ansiklopedi*, Istanbul 1993–95
Le Corbusier, *Journey to the East*, Paris 1966
Mango, C, *Byzanz*, Stuttgart 1986
Mango, C, *Istanbul, city of seven hills*, Istanbul 1994
Mimarlık Dergiler, Istanbul

Müller-Wiener, W, *Bildlexikon zur Topographie Istanbuls*, Tübingen
    1977
Observatoire Urbain d'Istanbul, *Lettres d'information*, Istanbul
Odenthal, J, *Istanbul, Bursa und Erdine*, Cologne 1990
Process Architecture 93, 'Turkey: pilgrimage to cities', Tokyo 1990
Restle, M, *Kunstführer Istanbul*, Stuttgart 1976
Trialog 49, *Istanbul Habitat*, Karlsruhe 1996
Yapı Endustri Merkezi Magazins, Istanbul

Glossary

BEDESTEN masonry building, usually in the centre of a market, where goods could be locked away at night

CAMEKÂN anteroom of a Turkish bath

CAMİ mosque

ÇARŞI market

ÇEŞME fountain

CUMBA projecting balcony, bay window

DARUŞŞİFA hospital

DERSHANE lecture hall

DOLMUŞ public taxi

GECEKONDU self-built or illegal housing

GÖBEKTAŞI raised marble slab for massages in Turkish bath

HAMAM Turkish bath

HAN inn for travellers, sometimes with stores and workshops attached

HARARET steam room in Turkish bath

HAREM women's part of house

İMARET public kitchen for the poor

KASIR small palace

KERVANSARAY accommodation for travellers

KİTAPLIK library

KONAK mansion

KÖŞK pavilion, villa

KÜLLİYE pious foundation made up of religious or philanthropic institutions attached to a mosque

MEDRESE school or theological college

MİHRAB prayer niche indicating the direction of Mecca

ŞADIRVAN fountain for ritual ablutions

SARAY palace

SEBİL fountain house from which water is served by an attendant
SEDİR divan
SELAMLIK men's part of house
ŞELSEBİL musical fountain
SICAKLIK steam room in Turkish bath
SOFA central hallway and main living space in an Ottoman house
SOĞUKLUK cool room in Turkish bath
TIMARHANE insane asylum
TÜRBE mausoleum
VAKIF pious foundation
YALI Bosphorus mansion

Using this book

This guide is divided into nine sections, each covering an area of Istanbul in which there are buildings of interest.

The easiest way to get to the different sections is by taxi (which is not expensive); once within a section, most of the buildings listed can be reached on foot. It is helpful to mention a nearby hotel or mosque to the taxi driver as many cannot read maps. It is more common to describe the route than the destination.

For those who want to use public transport, there are buses and a few trams. These are very cheap but inconvenient as stops are far apart and buses are often crowded. Buy tickets from a ticket office or bookstall in the street, usually located near the stops, and put your ticket into the box beside the driver on entering. Alternatively use a *dolmuş* – a public taxi that drives a specific route. Fares are listed at *dolmuş* stands.

Ferries leave from the Galata bridge quays. Ferries on the upstream side of the bridge go up the Golden Horn as far as Eyüp; ferries for Üsküdar, Kadıköy and the Princes' Isles leave from the downstream side of the bridge; ferries up the Bosphorus leave from the quay on the right bank of the Golden Horn downstream from the bridge. Special tour tickets allow you to use any ferry in the course of a day, breaking your journey as often as you wish.

The AZ Istanbul Street Atlas and RV Verlag Istanbul map are both very useful.

1 **Stamboul**
2 **Beyoğlu**
3 **Şişli**
4 **Beşiktaş**
5 **Bosphorus European Side**
6 **Bosphorus Asian Side**
7 **Üsküdar and Kadıköy**
8 **Princes' Isles**

Bosphorus

Sea of Marmara

Stamboul

Theodosian land wall
İstanbul Surları

Driving from Istanbul airport into the city through the chaotic industrial zones and satellite towns, you suddenly become aware of a line of massive, regular, old stone blocks – the city wall.

The wall, some 20 kilometres long, consisted of a land wall which marked the western edge of Stamboul and a sea wall which extended along the coast of the Sea of Marmara. Originally the two sections met, but the remains of the connecting wall were removed during the construction of the motorway in the late 1950s.

The land wall was built in the reign of Theodosius II (408–50) by his prefect Anthemius. It protected the most vulnerable side of the 14 square kilometres of Byzantium, stretching from the Marmara coast to the older wall of the colony of Blachernae (near Tekfur Sarayı), of which little remained. Damaged during several earthquakes and rebuilt many times, it was of strategical use for about 1000 years and continued to define the city's western edge until the middle of the twentieth century. This fortification was the most important of late antiquity and even in its present ruinous state it bears testimony to the grandeur of fifth-century military architecture.

The sea wall was about 8 kilometres long. Large parts of it were destroyed by the building of the railways in 1873. The land wall is about 6.5 kilometres long and consists of three elements: the moat; the outer wall, with its alternating square and crescent-shaped towers; and the main inner wall. This last has 96 square or polygonal towers at 50- to 75-metre intervals. It is about 11 metres high and 4.8 metres thick and consists of a rubble core between two facing walls of dressed stone. Layers of five courses of brick, laid at intervals of between seven and eleven courses of dressed stone, firmly bind the structure.

Recently the remains of the wall received a new lease of life. In 1985

Anthemius 413, restored 1986–93

Anthemius 413, restored 1986–93

Stamboul was included on the World Heritage List and a year later, with support from UNESCO, a project to restore the land wall and city gates was launched by the municipality of Istanbul. The area to be developed was divided into several parts, each of which was assigned to a team of architects, archaeologists and contractors. The result was that different sections were restored in different ways and with varying degrees of success – in some sections, for instance, the restoration has been archaeologically insensitive, using the wrong materials and adding inappropriate new parts.

A team of specialists from Istanbul Technical University (Z and M Ahunbay and others) restored the southern part of the land wall, from the first tower north of Kennedy Caddesi to the section between the fourth and fifth towers. They limited their intervention to a minimum, simply strengthening the existing fabric to enable it to resist moderate earthquakes and the damaging effects of climate and pollution.

The Ottoman fortification of Yedikule (1457–8) at the southern end of the wall and the palace of Tekfur Sarayı further north in Arcı Bey are both worth a visit.

ADDRESS land wall: from Ayvansaray to Yedikule parallel to Belgrat Caddesi; sea wall: Kennedy Caddesi parallel to Marmara shore TRANSPORT train to Yedikule, bus 28, 28T, to Topkapı or Edirnekapı ACCESS open

Anthemius 413, restored 1986–93

Anthemius 413, restored 1986–93

Church of St Stephen of the Bulgars

Bulgar Kilisesi

The Bulgarian church of St Stephen is an example of gothic revivalism with neo-romanesque details. Situated on the waterfront of the Golden Horn, it is made entirely of cast iron – inside and out – including the 'carved' ornamentation.

Different sources give different accounts of the building of the church. The most convincing, discovered in two Austrian journals by Mete Tapan and Hasan Kuruyazıcı and published in the Turkish architectural magazine *yapı*, claims that when the idea of replacing the priest's house and timber church that stood on the site with a larger church was put forward in 1890, it was decided to design a cast-iron rather than a stone structure because of the poor quality of the soil. A competition was to be organised, but in the mean time the Ottoman architect Housep Aznavour (1853–1935) drew up a preliminary design. His scheme was accepted and the contract to manufacture the church was awarded to an Austrian firm. In 1895 the building was erected temporarily in Vienna to check its parts before being disassembled and shipped in sections via the Danube and Black Sea to Istanbul.

It is thought that the church was inaugurated in 1898. Its architect, an Armenian by origin, is known to have studied in Rome and to have designed other buildings in Istanbul.

ADDRESS Vapur İskelesi Caddesi, Balat, Fener, Fatih
TRANSPORT bus 99, 99A, 399B, 399C or 399D to Balat
ACCESS open

Housep Aznavour 1898

Housep Aznavour 1898

Greek school of higher education
Rum Erkek Lisesi

When conjuring up of the skyline of Stamboul, the silhouettes of the vast mosques on the city's hilltops are first to come to mind. But there is another remarkable building which from a distance appears to be a church: the Greek grammar school for boys, now a Turkish public school. Located on an exposed site overlooking the Fener (lighthouse) district, the building opens up to the Golden Horn, offering a marvellous view of the harbour from its playground.

Istanbul was a multi-denominational city at least until the foundation of the Turkish Republic in 1923 and was very important for Orthodox Christianity. Fener was a prosperous Greek neighbourhood that grew up around the Greek Orthodox patriarchate in Sadrazam Ali Paşa Caddesi, established at the beginning of the seventeenth century. But until the first decades of the nineteenth century, the presence of non-Muslim structures on the city's skyline and the addition of towers and domes to Christian churches were forbidden (see Church of St Mary Draperis, page 148). Despite its relatively humble function as a school, this building, constructed after the restrictions were eased, was obviously intended as a symbol of the Greek power and presence in the city.

With its rich ornamental brickwork, the school is an example of historical eclecticism. The façade consists of grey-plastered panels surrounded by an apparently structural brick frame. A projecting, heavily profiled attic emphasises the mighty proportions of the construction. The symmetrical wings flank an octagonal tower which is extended by a dome with a lantern.

ADDRESS 36 Sancaktar Yokuşu Sokak, Fener, Fatih
ACCESS playground weekdays until 14.00, inside with permission

Dimadis 1880

Stamboul

Dimadis 1880

Women's library
Kadın Kütüphanesi

Built originally for an influential Greek family, this imposing mansion would have stood in contrast with the small timber houses that surrounded it.

The mansion consists of two two-storey cubes of different sizes. Each contains a single large room on each floor, while the lower one also houses the narrow entrance hall and staircase. Each of the six rooms is roofed by a brick barrel vault. One cube contains the library on the ground floor and reading room on the first floor, the other children's facilities and administration. The construction is alternate courses of dressed stone and brick. The windows originally had brick arches, later replaced by natural stone ties.

The restoration is modest and sensitive, maintaining the character of the original. Outside, the architect has provided seating in the form of an amphitheatre opposite the entrance in front of the Golden Horn, so the library acts as a kind of stage. The project is the first women's library in Turkey and its frequent use bears witness to its success.

Other buildings restored by Bektaş include the post office next to the library; Özbekler Tekkesi, a Dervish monastery in Üsküdar; and Turyap Genel Müdürlüğü, an art deco building in Arnavutköy.

ADDRESS Abdülezel Paşa Caddesi, Fener, Fatih
(telephone 0212 534 95 50)
TRANSPORT bus 99, 99A, 399B, 399C, 399D to Balat
ACCESS Tuesday, Thursday, Friday 10.00–19.00; Monday, Saturday, Sunday 13.00–19.00

eighteenth century, restoration Cengiz Bektaş 1988

eighteenth century, restoration Cengiz Bektaş 1988

Church of the Pantocrator
Molla Zeyrek Camii

Situated high above Atatürk Bulvarı, the beautiful monastery complex of the Pantocrator is one of the most important surviving Byzantine sanctuaries in the city.

The complex was originally made up of a monastery (now disappeared) and two parallel churches with a chapel between them and an exterior vestibule that was the most monumental since that at Haghia Sophia (see page 88). The monastery and the south church (1118–24) were founded by the Empress Eirene; the north church (completed c. 1143), chapel and exterior vestibule were built after her death by her husband Emperor John II Comnenus. The chapel – the last of the three surviving buildings to be constructed – was intended as a mausoleum for the tombs of the Comneni dynasty. The interiors, with their mosaics and marble floors, probably continued to be worked on until the death of John's son and successor Manuel I in 1180.

Both churches follow the same four-column plan, with a central dome, triple apse and an interior vestibule with a gallery. One enters the complex through a portal in the middle of the exterior vestibule and goes through one of five doors into the lower inner vestibule of the south church. The south church towers above the chapel and smaller north church. The chapel is highly irregular in form in order to fit between the two existing churches.

ADDRESS İbadethane Sokağı, Zeyrek, Fatih
TRANSPORT bus 77B, 83E, 99, 99A, 399H to Unkapı
ACCESS none

Social Security Agency complex

İstanbul İhtiyarık Sigortası Müdürlüğü

The Social Security Agency complex, located in the historic district of Zeyrek, was awarded an Ağa Khan Award for Architecture in 1986. Its architect, Sedad Hakkı Eldem, taught, researched and practised architecture for over 50 years and is one of the most important architectural figures in contemporary Turkey. His work focuses on the dialectic between the traditional and the contemporary and is rooted in both regionalism and international-style modernism.

This project, a complex of shops, offices and a clinic, is exemplary in the way it harmonises with the scale, character and topography of its site. The long elevation is fragmented by using blocks of different sizes and heights interspersed with open spaces. Each of the blocks has a reinforced-concrete frame, clearly distinguished from the infill walls with their vertically proportioned windows (an Eldem trademark) that together with the ceramic tiles and overhanging eaves make reference to traditional Ottoman architecture. The window style is continued throughout, relating to the architecture of the boulevard in front as well as to the surrounding timber houses and nearby Byzantine Church of the Pantocrator (see page 40).

The spine of the project is a double-height interior street connected to the blocks from the inside. This, together with the steps that link the boulevard with the Zeyrek slope above, makes reference to the open and covered streets characteristic of the Istanbul vernacular.

ADDRESS Atatürk Bulvarı, Zeyrek, Fatih
TRANSPORT bus 77B, 86B to Müze
ACCESS open

Sedad Hakkı Eldem 1962–4

Sedad Hakkı Eldem 1962–4

Museum of Cartoons and Humour
Türk Karikatür ve Mizah Müzesi

The museum was originally a *külliye* made up of a *medrese, sebil* and *türbe* for its founder, Gazanfer Ağa. It was completed by Davut Ağa – successor to Sinan as chief of the imperial architects – in 1599, the year of his death. The complex is a public statement of the status of its patron, the rich and powerful chief of the white eunuchs under Mehmet III.

The mix of public and private spaces in the complex is expressed in its plan and façade. The polygonal domed *sebil* with its overhanging eaves is located at the corner of the site, where it can offer shade and water to passers-by. By contrast the *medrese,* a centre of concentrated private study, presents a closed façade – adorned by repeated chimneys and cupolas – to the boulevard. The mausoleum and graveyard are semi-public in nature, protected against the urban environment only by open grilles.

After its restoration in 1944–5, the complex became the Municipal Museum. This was transferred to Yıldız palace in 1988 and the building was restored again to open as the Museum of Cartoons and Humour. The museum consists of an archive of documents relating to former and contemporary cartoonists (Turkish and foreign), a library containing international periodicals and publications, permanent and temporary exhibition space, a studio for an artist in residence, and a café. Home to numerous conferences, events and video shows, the originally private *medrese* has become a public, contemporary space that nevertheless respects its historical setting.

ADDRESS Atatürk Bulvarı, Saraçhanebaşı, Fatih
TRANSPORT bus 77B, 86B to Müze
ACCESS open daily 9.00–17.00; library closed Saturdays and Sundays

Davut Ağa 1599

Stamboul

Davut Ağa 1599

Aqueduct of Valens

Bozdoğan Kemeri

The aqueduct is the only remaining section of the water-supply system constructed in the inner city by the Emperor Valens between about 368 and 373. Today it forms a memorable backdrop to the chaotic traffic of Atatürk Bulvarı and a monumental bridge between two quarters of the city.

The aqueduct consists of a sequence of about 60 one- and two-storey arches, built of roughly hewn limestone. It is 920 metres long (originally 971 metres) and has a maximum height of 26.5 metres. Traffic flows under six of its arches.

The aqueduct contains two water channels at a gradient of 1:1000 and was capable of transporting 19,000 cubic metres of water per day. After the Ottoman conquest it supplied the Eski (Old) and Topkapı palaces with water. An upward slope between the forty-seventh and fifty-first arches, necessitating the pumping of the water, is a puzzle to historians: some believe it to be the result of an earthquake, others that a section of the aqueduct was deliberately removed by Süleyman to give an uninterrupted view of the Şehzade mosque.

In use until the late nineteenth century, the aqueduct has recently been restored using artificial stone to match the original porous stone, which could not be found in the required quantity and dimensions. The brick paving of the top to provide protection against the weather, begun in the Ottoman period, has also been completed.

ADDRESS Atatürk Bulvarı, Saraçhanebaşı, Fatih
RESTORATION ADVISER Professor Doğan Kuban
CONTRACTOR Pakerler Construction Company
TRANSPORT bus 77B, 86B to Müze

Stamboul

368–73

Istanbul city hall

Belediye Sarayı

Located near the aqueduct of Valens and opposite the Şehzade mosque, the city hall introduced the architecture of the international style into the heart of old Istanbul – a modern stranger in a traditional environment.

Nevzat Erol proposed an L-shaped complex oriented towards Atatürk Bulvarı. Like most entries to the competition, his scheme consisted of an office tower attached to a lower council block. The construction of the whole complex uses a concrete frame with brick infill, with façades based on a strict grid system.

The council block is a two-storey rectangular building containing a multi-purpose foyer and exhibition space, the mayor's office and the council meeting chamber. The entrance has a projecting canopy; the meeting chamber is covered by a hyperbolic cross-vault, giving the interior space, which is enriched with 1950s detailing, an interesting, steep profile. Though references to regional architecture are not strikingly obvious, one can perhaps detect a relationship between this vault roof and the traditional mosque dome, as well as a connection with the architecture of Le Corbusier, who was influenced by the form of Istanbul's mosques following a visit here in 1911. The eight-storey office tower has a single vault with a floating roof on top. The two buildings, connected by bridges, are decorated with panels of small coloured tiles.

Ponds and benches were installed in an attempt to create an urban space between the two blocks – a fruitless task in view of the openness of the surroundings and lack of neighbouring buildings.

Also worth seeing is the international-style Hilton Hotel (1952) on Cumhuriyet Caddesi, Harbiye by SOM and Sedad Hakkı Eldem.

ADDRESS Şehzadebaşı Caddesi, Kalenderhane, Eminönü
ACCESS with guide only (telephone 0212 512 55 00)

Nevzat Erol 1953

Stamboul

Nevzat Erol 1953

Textile market
İstanbul Manifaturacılar Çarşısı

The complex was the winning entry to a limited competition for a textile market. The brief was for 1100 shops, each between 80 and 100 square metres in size, with auxiliary facilities. The site, an 800-metre-long strip, runs parallel to the traffic-laden Atatürk Bulvarı in an area packed with some 30 historic buildings, including the Sülemaniye and Fatih mosques on the hills on either side.

The architects are well known as progressive modernists. Since 1954 (nowadays without Hepgüler) they have built factories (for instance, the Bayer-Pharmaceutical plant in Topkapı, near E5 Oto Yolu, 1967–70), high-rise blocks and large projects all over Turkey. Their best scheme is perhaps the Corbusian Turkish embassy in New Delhi (1962–3 and 1979–83).

Here, they proposed a functional solution that provided a variety of spaces. The proportions mediate between the organic urban texture of the historic district and the large complexes on the opposite side of the boulevard. The scheme, based on a 5 by 5-metre grid, consists of six blocks containing a total of 180,000 square metres of floor space. The complex provides a buffer zone between the historic district and the busy boulevard, with pedestrians within totally separated from the traffic outside. Shops are arranged around pedestrian courtyards or along the walkways that connect them. All the blocks are oriented towards the Sülemaniye and the complex is interrupted in the middle by the Şebsefa Hatun mosque, maintaining the visual link between the historic religious buildings. A courtyard with a fountain between the first and second blocks has an impressive view towards the Sülemaniye.

Taking advantage of the natural slope of the site, the buildings are arranged in terraces, facilitating pedestrian circulation. A service road running parallel to the boulevard provides parking spaces and access for

Tekeli, Sisa & Hepgüler 1959

Tekeli, Sisa & Hepgüler 1959

deliveries. Alleys link the service road with Atatürk Bulvarı.

The buildings are of exposed concrete with non-loadbearing walls clad in travertine. Red ('Ottoman pink') pre-cast mosaic grilles protect the glazed façades from the sun. Instead of varying the materials, the architects relied on the use of a limited range of elements – cantilevers, stairs and grilles – to provide enrichment. Occasionally contemporary mosaics and sculptures are integrated.

Recent alterations mean that some of the subtlety of the complex has been lost: grilles have been removed and the travertine plastered and painted green. Nevertheless, the convincing treatment of external and internal space is still worth seeing.

Also visit Vefa-Bozacısı (1876) at 102 Katıp Çelebi Caddesi/Cemal Yener Tosyalı Caddesi, Vefa/Eminönü, a bar open all day long where you can buy only two things: Boza, a delicious gooey drink, and vinegar.

ADDRESS Atatürk Bulvarı, Vefa, Eminönü
TRANSPORT bus to Unkapanı or Müze
ACCESS open

Tekeli, Sisa & Hepgüler 1959

Stamboul

Tekeli, Sisa & Hepgüler 1959

Hotel Merit Antique

Kemalettin Bey (1870–1927), together with Vedat Tek (see page 112), was the acknowledged leader of the first national architectural movement (1912–29), in which architects aimed to combine elements from the country's Ottoman heritage with contemporary western building technology to create an appropriate national architecture. Bey was the most influential architect working in the new capital of Ankara from its establishment in 1923 until his death, not only because of his numerous buildings – mosques, mausoleums, offices, prisons, hospitals, railway stations and some 40 schools – but also because of his influence in disseminating the principles of a new national design. Having trained under Jachmund at the German-influenced School of Civil Engineering in Istanbul and at the Charlottenburg Technical University in Berlin, he became chief architect to the Ministry of War and then in 1909 to the Ministry of Pious Foundations. In the course of the restoration work involved in the latter position, he analysed the principles of Ottoman architecture and from them developed his own style.

During the First World War Istanbul suffered a great fire which increased the city's housing shortage. The Hotel Merit Antique was originally built as the Harikzedeğan (fire victims') apartments, intended to house 124 low-income families, on a site belonging to the Ministry of Pious Foundations. In contrast with the traditional inward-looking Muslim housing, the four six-storey blocks with their communal laundry and service facilities, courtyards with open staircases, and integrated shops at ground- and first-floor levels – perhaps showing the influence of Bey's time in Berlin – were designed to encourage social interaction. Their popularity tells of their architect's success in recognising contemporary social changes.

The scheme was one of the first examples of reinforced-concrete

Kemalettin Bey 1919–22

Kemalettin Bey 1919–22

construction in the country. But with its traditional symmetrical façades with bay windows and curved elements above the attic windows and two-storey shops within segmental arches, it also attempted to harmonise with the nearby eighteenth-century mosque of Laleli.

Considering that this is one of the most important works of the first national architectural movement, it was treated very badly when it was taken over by the hotel chain. While the exterior is more or less in its original state, the interior has been destroyed by the introduction of unsuitable materials and colours. The idea of vertical circulation via open courtyards has been spoiled by adding a tasteless roof construction and introducing air conditioning. Although the idea of converting the complex into a hotel was a good one, the way it has been realised leaves much to be desired.

ADDRESS Hotel Merit Antique Istanbul (formerly the Ramada Hotel), 226 Ordu Caddesi, Laleli, Eminönü (telephone 0212 513 93 00)
RESTORATION Net-Holding
TRANSPORT tram or bus 35, 86B to Laleli
ACCESS open

Kemalettin Bey 1919–22

Stamboul

Kemalettin Bey 1919–22

Beyazit Square
Beyazit Meydanı

Beyazit Square is the only remaining ancient square in Istanbul, albeit incomplete. Parts of the existing square correspond with the Byzantine Forum Tauri or Forum of Theodosius I (379–95), though since that time the space has had a chequered urban history.

Immediately after the Ottoman conquest of 1453, Mehmet II erected his palace, the Eski Sarayı, next to the square. In 1501–6 the Beyazit mosque – the oldest surviving Ottoman imperial mosque and a prototype for classical Ottoman mosque architecture – was built opposite the palace entrance and a convincing rectangular urban space was created by the addition of the Beyazit *medrese*.

In the second half of nineteenth century the Eski Sarayı was demolished to make way for a new Ministry of War complex (1866–70, by Auguste Bourgeois), which now houses the University of Istanbul. The complex's neo-Islamic gate with its two flanking pavilions was angled at 45 degrees to the south-easterly orientation of the mosque, and the square lost its density. In 1926 a neo-baroque, French-style urban plan was adopted with a central avenue of trees and elliptical pond, completely disregarding the existing fabric and topography. In 1957 the green space was sacrificed to make way for extra streets.

Architects such as Turgut Cansever have made proposals to restore the spatial identity and historic scale of the square and an urban-design competition was launched in 1965, but the results were not implemented. Finally, Beyazit Square was converted into a pedestrian area – the first of its kind in Turkey. Today it is a crowded public space, accommodating business of all kinds.

ADDRESS Beyazit, Eminönü
TRANSPORT tram to Beyazit

University of Istanbul observatory

Observatoryum

The observatory was built for the Department of Astronomy and Space Science of the University of Istanbul. The head of department at the time, German astronomer Findlay-Freundlich, had worked in Erich Mendelsohn's Einstein Tower in Potsdam (1920–1).

The building, approximately 20 metres by 10 metres in plan, was originally symmetrical. The central cylindrical tower, containing the telescope on the top floor reached by a spiral staircase from the entrance below, is flanked by single-storey wings containing work and seminar rooms. The hall and main staircase are on axis with the tower. The two-storey central section gives access to the roofs of the wings, which form observation terraces. The tower has a copper-clad dome with a sliding opening for the telescope. For protection against vibration, the telescope has its own foundations.

The influence of the modern movement is apparent in the horizontal façade and the glazed skeleton that wraps the staircase. However, the symmetrical 'butterfly' plan is more reminiscent of the traditional Ottoman cruciform plan (see page 234). Although not stringently modern, the building is among the first examples of international-style Turkish architecture – and is charming too.

In 1958 supplementary spaces were added: a gangway leading to an instrument-storage room on the main axis and a long corridor with administration, visitors' and seminar rooms at each end at right angles to this axis. As a result, the position of the main entrance was changed. A freestanding library was also added. Despite a successful attempt to employ the same architectural language as the original, the extended complex lost its clarity and compactness.

Also worth seeing on campus is the 50-metre-high Beyazit tower, designed in 1828 as a fire-watch station by Senekerim Balyan (see page

Muallim A Hikmet Holtay 1934–6

Muallim A Hikmet Holtay 1934–6

246), which is reminiscent of the minaret of the Nusretiye mosque (1822–6) in Tophane/Beyoğlu. The main university building, formerly the Ministry of War complex, is by French architect Auguste Bourgeois and dates from 1866–70, with a 1934 extension and alteration by the Swiss architect Malche. Leaving the campus, you should look at the new university in Ordu Caddesi, built in the 1950s by Emin Onat and Sedad Hakkı Eldem (see page 42). The monumental blocks bear witness to the influence of German émigré architect Paul Bonatz, who taught at Istanbul's School of Civil Engineering from 1946 to 1954.

ADDRESS İstanbul Üniversitesi Fen Fakültesi, Beyazit, Eminönü (telephone 0212 522 35 97; fax 0212 519 08 34)
TRANSPORT tram to Beyazit
ACCESS open, but it is advisable to ask permission

Muallim A Hikmet Holtay 1934–6

Süleymaniye mosque
Süleymaniye Camii

The Süleymaniye was the fourth imperial mosque to be built in Istanbul after the Fatih (1463–70), Beyazit (1501–6) and Selim I (1522) complexes. While the simplest mosques are small buildings with a single minaret and a small forecourt containing the tomb of the founder, the mosques of the Ottoman sultans are impressive structures with several minarets, set in their own outer courts and walled gardens surrounded by a large complex of buildings that form part of the pious foundation (*külliye*).

Inside the imperial mosques is a private lodge where the sultan prayed with the principal members of his harem; immediately outside is a monumental forecourt surrounded on three sides by a domed arcade with a central fountain for ritual ablutions before prayer. Within the boundaries of the walled garden is a *türbe* for the sultan and his relatives. Outside the walls is the *külliye*, consisting of trade and charitable institutions including a *medrese* (secondary school or specialist college), *daruşşifa* (hospital), *imaret* (public kitchen), *kervansaray* (accommodation for travellers) and *hamam* (baths). These huge complexes were expressions of the power of the Ottoman sultans, and with Süleyman the Magnificent the development reached its height. Economically, the imperial mosques functioned in a similar manner to medieval monasteries, gaining income from a mixture of land ownership and trade. The Süleymaniye owns 200 villages, several mills and two islands and gains further revenue from the *hamam*s, the rent of shops and the sale of goods. The *imaret* caters for the poor of the city area and for all those who work in the *külliye* – more than 800 people. Today the estate is managed by the government.

This complex, providing a home and workplace for hundreds of people, is a small city in itself. But whereas traditional Islamic cities are made up of arbitrarily placed timber houses with no orthogonal street

Sinan 1550–7

Sinan 1550–7

grids or monumental squares – expressing the Islamic belief that everything on earth is temporary in nature – the mosques and *külliyes* are usually orthogonally composed and built of monumental stone. The grey, fine-grained sandstone gives them a unified appearance that distinguishes them from their surroundings. The interiors, with their red carpets and walls decorated with green and blue tiles or ornamental paintings, belie the austerity of the exteriors.

Sinan (c. 1490–1588) was for half a century chief of the imperial architects, serving under Süleyman and his immediate successors Selim II and Murat III. His list of over 300 works, including some 130 mosques, represents the golden age of the Ottoman empire and his Selimiye mosque in Edirne, designed when he was 85, is the acknowledged masterpiece of Ottoman architecture. Born of Christian parents, he was taken into the sultan's service (as part of an annual levy of Christian youths) when he was about 21 and served as a military engineer in the Janissaries. As chief of the imperial architects, he developed the typology of the mosque to include a single domed square, a repeated domed square, a double space with ancilliary side spaces and numerous variations on a central dome surrounded by half domes with domed side aisles. His interest in urban design ensured that his buildings took full advantage of the topography of their sites and responded to the context of the surrounding city. For two centuries the construction of mosques remained under the spell of Sinan and there was little attempt at innovation until the eighteenth century. He was allowed to build his own tomb on a corner of the Süleymaniye site – the only architect honoured in this way.

The Süleymaniye complex (1560–75) is built on Istanbul's highest hill, in accordance with the Islamic ideal that religious buildings should exploit the topography of the city to impress from a distance: the immense

Stamboul

Sinan 1550–7

dome seen from Galata dominates the city above the Golden Horn. Sinan also left plenty of space around the mosque to ensure its appreciation close to; only Süleyman's *türbe*, the largest and most impressive of its time, and the *türbe* of his first wife Roxelana are located near the mosque, at the back of the garden.

The mosque stands in the middle of a garden surrounded by a low wall. The *imaret* and *kervansaray* are opposite the main entrance and in the corner is the *darüşşifa*. The *medrese*s are located in the side streets. The main entrance had to be at the north-west of the site because of the south-eastern orientation of Mecca, which means it is only indirectly accessible from the city centre. The entry is designed so that one does not see the impressive front view of the mosque until the last moment. The grandeur of the mosque is offset by the subdued simplicity of the buildings of the *külliye*, creating an appropriate harmony of function and form.

Of all Sinan's buildings, the Sülemaniye is most similar to Haghia Sophia (see page 88) in plan and spatial organisation: a central main dome supported by semidomes to the east and west. But the Sülemaniye is based on the Islamic ideal of creating an impression of infinite space, so the division in the basilica between nave and side aisles is suppressed in favour of transparency and long views. The combination of different types of windows creates a diffuse light. But the pillars interrupt the fluidity of the space, and for this reason Sinan soon abandoned the four-pier plan for a centrally organised structure (see Rüstem Paşa mosque, page 118).

ADDRESS Süleymaniye Caddesi, Eminönü
TRANSPORT tram to Beyazit
ACCESS open

Stamboul

Sinan 1550–7

Sinan 1550–7

Süleymaniye medreses

The Süleymaniye *külliye* originally contained six *medrese*s: the Evvel (first), Sani (second) and Tıp Medresesi (medical school) on one side of the mosque and the Salis (third), Rabı (fourth) and Mülazimler (for preparatory students) on the opposite side. Each of the four principal *medrese*s was dedicated to the teachings of one of the four orthodox schools of Islamic law; the medical school, once the foremost in the empire, has been largely replaced by a modern concrete building housing a maternity clinic.

The plan of the *medrese* changed little from the first Ottoman examples until the eighteenth century. Traditionally the buildings consisted of a network of domed cells arranged around three or four sides of a square arcaded courtyard. Interrupting the cells on one side would be the *dershane* or lecture hall – a larger domed room used for teaching and prayer. Often the *medrese* site would also contain the *türbe* of the founder and a *sebil* open to the public. A notable exception to this standard plan is Sinan's Rüstem Paşa *medrese* (1550, see page 118), which has an octagonal courtyard surrounded by 22 domed cells and a projecting south-facing *dershane*, with triangular washrooms and offices at the corners so that the complex still reads from the outside as a square.

The *medrese*s of the Süleymaniye *külliye* are the most interesting and beautiful of all Sinan's educational buildings. The Evvel and Sani *medrese*s on the south side of the mosque are built as mirror images of each other, separated only by an alley. They now house the Süleymaniye library, which contains some 30,000 manuscripts. The *daruşşifa* (hospital) stands on the corner at the same level, so viewed from this side the domes of the mosque appear to rise out of a series of smaller cupolas.

The Salis and Rabı *medrese*s are built on the steep northern slope of the Third Hill. Though the lower sides of their courtyards are raised on

Sinan 1550–7

Sinan 1550–7

high superstructures to accommodate the slope, with the Mülazimler tucked in below, the courtyards still slope down quite sharply. The cells along the sides are built on five different levels, connected by flights of steps. Between the identical Salis and Rabı *medrese*s is a courtyard with steps leading down to the Mülazimler. Viewed from the seaward side, the domes of these *medrese*s appear to lead up to the crowning glory of the mosque itself.

ADDRESS Süleymaniye Caddesi, Eminönü
TRANSPORT tram to Beyazit
ACCESS none

Sinan 1550–7

Sinan 1550–7

Covered bazaar
Kapalı Çarşısı

A covered bazaar was a feature of most of the cities of the Ottoman empire. Traditionally these were constructed around a *bedesten* (from *bez*, the Turkish word for 'cloth'), a masonry building that could be locked at night to protect cloth and other valuables to be traded. Most of the *bedesten*s were founded by grand vezirs in the fifteenth and sixteenth centuries and took the form of a rectangular hall roofed by several small domes, often connected to an *arasta* – a complex of small shops each between 4 and 10 metres square set on either side of an enclosed domed arcade with lockable doors at each end. Near or inside the bazaar there would also be several small mosques and fountains.

The Kapalı Çarşısı in Istanbul was established on its present site by Mehmet II shortly after the conquest. Though most of it has been destroyed by fire and earthquakes several times since (as early as 1547 and most recently in 1954), its appearance and structure are essentially the same as when it was first built. It has an area of 30.7 hectares, some 3000 shops, two *bedesten*s, 13 *han*s and a grid of more than 80 streets.

At the centre is the Old Bedesten, one of the few parts of the original structure to have survived. The hall with its 15 domes, each 7 metres in diameter, houses the most valuable goods on sale, as it would have done 500 years ago.

The modern version of the bazaar is the shopping centre. Given that Istanbul is a city with terrible traffic problems, shopping centres have become popular. Capitol on Bağlarbası Tophanelioğlu Caddesi in Üsküdar and Akmerkez in Etiler are two examples.

ADDRESS between Nuru Osmaniye Camii and Beyazit Camii, Eminönü
TRANSPORT tram to Beyazit or Çemberlitaş
ACCESS Monday to Saturday 8.00–19.00

1453–

1453–

Büyük Yeni inn

Büyük Yeni Han

The *han*s were inns that offered accommodation to travellers along the caravan or merchant routes between Europe and the far east. In the cities, *han*s often included small workshops for craftsmen and space where goods were bought and sold. The names of the *han*s – for instance, Kürkçu Hanı (Han of the Furriers) – indicate that many were dedicated to specific guilds of traders. They were usually founded by sultans or wealthy citizens and located near a mosque complex.

The typical Istanbul *han* is a three-storey rectangular building with a central courtyard. The ground floor had stables for the travellers' horses or camels, storerooms for the goods they had brought and workshops, while the upper floors contained sleeping cells opening on to galleries with stairs leading down to the courtyard.

The Büyük Yeni Han (literally Big New Han) was founded by Mustafa III and is the city's second-largest *han*, with 150 sleeping cells. The long narrow courtyard (85 by 15 metres) was unfortunately divided in half in the nineteenth century by a rough stone building. The most impressive features are the projecting bay windows on the upper levels of the alleyway façade.

Also look at Küçük Yeni Han, built under Mustafa III in the same street; Kürkçu Hanı (1467), the city's oldest *han*, in Mahmut Paşa Yokuşu; and Sinan's Rüstem Paşa Hanı (1544–50) south of Tersane Caddesi.

ADDRESS Çakmakçılar Yokuşu, Eminönü
TRANSPORT tram to Beyazit or Çemberlitaş
ACCESS open

Stamboul

1764

Column of Constantine
Çemberlitaş

From a distance you could mistake it for a chimney, but in fact the Column of Constantine, built at the centre of the elliptical Forum of Constantine to commemorate the dedication of the city as capital of the Roman empire, is Istanbul's most famous triumphal column and one of the few surviving monuments from Constantine's city. Çemberlitaş (literally 'hooped column'), located on Istanbul's second hill, was one of several monuments punctuating the main east–west route through the city, the *mese* ('porticoed avenue'), today's Divanyolu. The erection of honorary columns was a pagan tradition that continued for two centuries after Constantine (306–37). The emperor himself built three columns, one dedicated to his mother and two in his own honour.

The column was originally 50 metres high with a marble base on six steps and a shaft of ten porphyry drums topped by a capital supporting a statue of the emperor as Apollo. In 416 the column was damaged by an earthquake and in 418 iron hoops were placed around the junctions between the drums to try to stabilise it. A storm in 1105–6 overturned the statue, capital and three of the drums. Following a fire in 1779 the base and lowest drum were given a brick casing. The surface of the forum was 2.33 metres lower than today's street level and today what remains of the column stands at 34.8 metres high. Until the 1865 Hocapaşa fire, the column was surrounded by houses; afterwards a small triangular square was created around it.

Also look at the Column of Marcian (450–2), known locally as Kız Taşı ('maiden's column'), in Kıztaşı Caddesi, Saraçhane/Fatih.

ADDRESS Çemberlitaş, Eminönü
TRANSPORT tram to Çemberlitaş

Sultan Ahmet mosque (Blue mosque)
Sultan Ahmet Camii

Located opposite the monumental Byzantine church of Haghia Sophia (see page 88), this last of the great imperial mosques represents a final flourish of power and greatness before the decline of the power of the sultans and with it of Ottoman architecture. Built by Mehmet Ağa, a student of Sinan, for the young Sultan Ahmet I, the Blue mosque has the biggest courtyard of all the Ottoman mosques and the greatest number of minarets (six). Because of its location near the Topkapı palace (see page 92), most of the reigning sultans for the next 250 years used it for their weekly Friday noontime prayers and it ranks in importance with the Süleymaniye (see page 64) among Istanbul's religious monuments.

The courtyard, which is as large as the mosque itself, is in the classic style, bordered by a portico covered by 30 small domes. The façade with its repeated arches and columns gives a restful sense of symmetry and enclosure. The plan of the mosque is also classical – basically that of Sinan's Şehzade mosque (1548), with elements from the Yeni mosque designed by Davut Ağa in 1597 but not completed until 1663. The interior, with its dome supported on four massive piers, called 'elephant's feet', is huge and impressive, a testimony to Mehmet Ağa's engineering skills. The familiar quatrefoil plan is enlivened by the use of galleries on all sides.

Ahmet I was a great lover of tiles and over 21,000 were used for the section of wall between the two sets of windows alone. But the difficulties inherent in manufacturing so many means that they are of varying quality and better examples of tile decoration can be found in smaller buildings such as the Rüstem Paşa mosque (see page 118). The Blue mosque is lit by 260 windows which were originally glazed with coloured glass imported from Venice. It takes its popular name from the predominantly blue decoration of the domes and upper part of the structure.

Mehmet Ağa 1609–16

Stamboul

Mehmet Ağa 1609–16

In contrast with the huge, formally arranged *külliye*s of the Süleymaniye and Fatih mosques, the buildings of the complex surrounding the Blue mosque were organised more freely. Today only the *imaret*, primary school, *medrese* and *türbe* remain. The most important example of a *tımarhane* (asylum) after that of the Süleymaniye *külliye* was unfortunately destroyed in the nineteenth century together with the *kervansaray*, hospital and market.

A ramp at the north-east corner of the mosque leads to the imperial pavilion, connected by means of an internal passageway to the royal lodge within the mosque.

Stamboul

ADDRESS Sultanahmet, Eminönü
TRANSPORT tram to Sultanahmet
ACCESS open

Mehmet Ağa 1609–16

Stamboul

Mehmet Ağa 1609–16

Baths of Roxelana
Haseki Hürrem Hamamı (Aya Sofya Hamamı)

The œuvre of Sinan, chief of the imperial architects from 1538 until his death at the age of 97 in 1588, includes 32 *hamam*s, the masterpiece of which is the Haseki Hürrem Hamamı, built by Süleyman the Magnificent for his wife Haseki Hürrem (better known in the west as Roxelana). The hierarchic sequence of geometric elements in plan and elevation makes the complex a particularly intense spatial experience.

Although *hamam*s are generally introverted buildings in which the exterior is of little importance, the Haseki Hürrem Hamamı has an arresting external form created by the repeated module of a domed cube surmounted by a lantern. This repeated pattern reflects the plan of the interior and was also presumably an appropriate response to the density of the sixteenth-century urban surroundings, though today the *hamam* stands exposed, its interplay of rectilinear and curved forms clearly visible. Unusually for a double *hamam* (compare Çukurcuma baths, page 150), the separate male and female sections, which are usually arranged side by side or interlocked, are here placed end to end along a single axis. This produces a long narrow building (75 metres by 20 metres) appropriate for its narrow site. The men's entrance faces the apse of Haghia Sophia while the more modest women's entrance is at the opposite end.

The *camekân*s (anterooms for dressing and relaxing) at each end are fine square halls with marble fountains and lofty domes – as spacious as the interiors of many mosques (appropriately enough, since the *hamam* is a religious ritual as well as a pleasurable activity). The furnace room is located on the south elevation, shifting the axis of the *soğukluk*s (cool rooms) and *sıcaklık*s (steam rooms) slightly northwards. The *soğukluk*s are simple rectangular spaces with three domes with lavatories along their northern flank. The elegant *sıcaklık*s are octagonal domed chambers with

Sinan 1556–7

Sinan 1556–7

four niches and four recesses for depilation, each with three basins.

Today a connecting passageway has been built between the male and female sections and the *hamam* is used as a carpet shop. The carpets do not detract from the well-restored interior and the pleasant atmosphere.

Also worth seeing are the baroque Cağlaoğlu Hamamı (1741–2) on Prof. K İsmail Gürkan Caddesi, Cağlaoğlu – a bath with the male and female sections interlocked; and the Çemberlitaş Hamamı (1574–83), 8 Vezirhan Caddesi, Çemberlitaş, in which the male and female sections run side by side. Both are still in use.

Stamboul

ADDRESS Ayasofya Meydanı, Sultanahmet, Eminönü
TRANSPORT tram to Sultanahmet
ACCESS open 9.30–17.30; closed Tuesdays

Sinan 1556–7

Sinan 1556–7

Haghia Sophia

Aya Sofya

In the eyes of contemporaries, Haghia Sophia was a whim of the emperor; for later generations it has become a symbol of the golden age of the Byzantine empire and of the city of Istanbul itself.

The first church dedicated to Haghia Sophia, the Divine Wisdom, on the present site – a basilica with a timber roof – was completed in 360 by Constantine's son and successor Constantinius and was burned down in a riot in 404. A new church, built under Theodosius II and consecrated in 415, was burned down in the reign of Justinian in the Nika revolt of 532, during which many of the buildings on the first hill were destroyed. The present Hagia Sophia was begun as soon as the revolt ended and was completed almost six years later at the end of 537. Its architects were the physicist and mechanical engineer Anthemeus of Tralles and the mathematician Isidorus of Miletus.

Haghia Sophia was until the end of the Byzantine empire the Greek Orthodox cathedral of Constantinople and the scene of the country's most important ceremonies. It was stripped of all its sacred relics during the Latin occupation of 1204–61, when it served as the Roman Catholic cathedral. The day of the Ottoman conquest of 1453, Mehmet II ordered its immediate conversion into a mosque, and the first Muslim service, attended by the sultan, was held there the following Friday. The building remained a mosque until 1932, then after two years of renovation was opened as a museum in 1934.

The basic plan is that of a basilica roofed by an enormous dome, with two great semidomes to the east and west resting on secondary vaults that almost double the length of the nave. The main 'celestial dome' – some 30 metres in diameter with an inner surface of 40 ribs separated at their base by for 40 windows – is supported on four colossal piers. The many windows and columned arcades accentuate the transparency of the space.

Anthemeus of Tralles and Isidorus of Miletus 532–7

Anthemeus of Tralles and Isidorus of Miletus 532–7

The original dome was weakened by several earthquakes and eventually collapsed in 558, to be replaced by a dome with a slightly smaller base and steeper sides. Subsequent earthquakes led to another partial collapse in 1346, and though the church was reopened after reconstruction a decade later, it was seriously neglected and allowed to fall into disrepair during the last century of Byzantine rule.

Successive structural crises led to the addition of buttresses on all sides of the massive exterior. These were extended and the general fabric of the structure restored by the chief of the imperial architects Sinan in the mid-1570s, at which time he also added three new stone minarets to the brick one erected by Mehmet II after the conquest.

After 1400 years, the building's condition is remarkably good. As one of the city's principal imperial mosques, it was well looked after under Ottoman rule, the last noteworthy restoration before its transformation into a museum being that carried out by Swiss architects Gaspare and Giuseppe Fossati in 1847–9, when the mosaics, which had been plastered over during the conversion into a mosque, were uncovered.

The original building was flooded with light, which was reflected in the surface of the many gold mosaics; today's dark, mysterious interior is the result of the bricking-up of windows and the loss of much of the decoration. High points: the interior and, of course, the dome.

ADDRESS Sultanahmet, Eminönü
TRANSPORT tram to Sultanahmet
ACCESS open 9.30–16.30; closed Mondays

Stamboul

Anthemeus of Tralles and Isidorus of Miletus 532–7

Stamboul

Anthemeus of Tralles and Isidorus of Miletus 532–7

Topkapı palace
Topkapı Sarayı

The Topkapı palace – the imperial residence of the Ottoman sultans for some 300 years – is the most extensive piece of Ottoman secular architecture in existence and one of the city's most individual monuments. Its first buildings date from 1465 and its last from 1840, 13 years before Abdül Mecit I moved the imperial residence to the Dolmabahçe palace (see page 194) on the shores of the Bosphorus.

In contrast to European palaces, Topkapı is not a single monumental building; rather, it consists of a sequence of four courts which contain groups of low freestanding pavilions and landscaped gardens. Some sources explain this lack of monumentalism as following a tenet of Islamic religion whereby secular architecture – even the architecture of palaces – has to reflect the idea that everything secular on earth is temporary in nature, so the Topkapı pavilions are not constructed to be eternal like the stone-built mosques; their scale is small and they demonstrate no hierarchy of form and function. Others claim that the temporary character of the buildings is a continuation of the nomadic Ottoman tradition of living in tents.

Topkapı was as much a centre for the education of civil servants, the administration of the empire and the seat of government as an imperial residence. At its height it housed some 40,000 people. The conglomeration of buildings from different periods is located over an area of some 70 hectares at the east end of the peninsula, on the site of the former acropolis of Byzantium. The complex took full advantage of the existing topography, with the palace buildings constructed on the high ground and extensive gardens laid out on the slopes of the hill and the shore below.

The first of the Topkapı's four courts was the service area of the palace and was open to the public. It contained a hospital, a bakery (behind the blank wall on the right-hand side), a branch of the treasury and dormi-

1465–1840

tories for guards and servants as well as the Byzantine church of Haghia Eirene (537, rebuilt after 740), which was used as an arsenal, and the area of today's Gülhane park and Archaeological Museum (1896). Here too is the oldest remaining imperial pavilion, the Çinili Köşkü (1472), its strict cruciform plan a predecessor of many of Istanbul's later buildings. Near the far right-hand corner is a fountain flanked by two truncated pillars: the fountain was used by the chief executioner to wash his hands and sword after performing his duties; the heads of executed criminals would be displayed on the pillars.

The entrance gate to the second court (1524) marked the border between the area open to the public and the seat of government. Landscaped with cypresses, plane trees and rosebushes and containing peacocks, gazelles and other birds and animals, this court was devoted largely to the imperial Divan (Council of State and Justice) and the inner treasury. To the right is the large kitchen block which included accommodation for cooks and metal-workers, storerooms, a mosque and ten kitchens, each roofed by a dome with a ventilation chimney. At its height, about 5000 meals a day were cooked here. The kitchen complex was restored by Sinan after a fire in 1574.

The *harem* (1541 onwards) – an extensive complex of some 300 rooms on several levels with gardens and inner courtyards – connects the second and third courts. This introverted labyrinth included the private apartments of the sultan and his mother (valide sultan) and rooms for the young princes and the black eunuchs who were in charge of the *harem*, as well as the women's quarters or *harem* proper. The *harem* was added to over a long period of time, as can be seen from the different styles and scales of the architecture.

Most of the buildings flanking the third court were part of the palace

Stamboul

1465–1840

school, which provided a largely secular education designed to train likely young boys to administer the empire. The throne room (1514–20) and the library of Ahmet III (1718) stand in the centre.

The fourth court is a garden with terraces stepping down towards the tip of the peninsula. Pavilions dating from the seventeenth and eighteenth centuries are artfully integrated into the landscape, demonstrating the strong relationship between architecture and topography. The pavilions with their cruciform plans, bays, overhanging eaves and low windows provide a lexicon of Ottoman architectural elements. Across a road leading to the outer gardens is the last building to be added to the complex: the two-storey western-style Mecidiye pavilion by Sarkis Balyan (1840), which now houses a restaurant.

Not to be missed, the Topkapı Sarayı demonstrates the development of an Ottoman complex from the Ottoman conquest of Istanbul in the fifteenth century to the westernised period of the nineteenth century.

ADDRESS Babıhumayün Caddesi, Sultanahmet, Eminönü
RESTORATION ARCHITECTS İlban Öz, Mualla Eyuboğlu-Anhegger (*harem*) and others
TRANSPORT tram to Sultanahmet
ACCESS open 9.30–17.00; closed Tuesdays (telephone 0212 512 04 80)

1465–1840

Istanbul library
Istanbul Kitaplığı

The Turkish Touring and Automobile Society under the directorship of Dr Çelik Gülersoy is committed to the promotion of Turkish culture. Since 1971, the society has used the revenue from issuing import documents for cars to restore and convert historic buildings which it acquires from the government for this purpose. Unfortunately the society has recently lost its income as a result of policy changes and the future of many of its buildings is threatened.

Several of the severely delapidated timber houses in Soğukçeşme Sokağı, between the Topkapı palace and Haghia Sophia, were completely rebuilt by the society in the 1980s. Because of present-day building regulations and lack of timber, the reconstructions mostly use brick and concrete. The largest of these houses was converted into a library to house Gülersoy's 7000-piece collection of books about Istanbul, some of which date from the sixteenth century. The façade of the two-storey mansion has a ground floor rendered in yellow plaster with yellow timber on the upper floor and asymmetrical bay windows supported on brackets. Although Gülersoy's conversions are sometimes controversial, the changes he introduces always work within a traditional idiom.

Around the corner is another of his projects, the Yeşil Ev hotel and restaurant, and next door is the Sarnıç (cistern). Also worth a visit are the hotel and restaurant at 5 Kabasakal Caddesi, Sultanahmet, and the Istanbul handicrafts centre next door; Emirgân park; and Yıldız park (see page 208).

ADDRESS Soğukçeşme Sokağı, Sultanahmet, Eminönü
TRANSPORT tram to Sultanahmet
ACCESS by permission (telephone 0212 512 57 30)

Stamboul

restoration Turkish Touring and Automobile Society 1980s

Stamboul

restoration Turkish Touring and Automobile Society 1980s

Yerebatan Sarayı cistern

Gardens and green spaces laid out in unpopulated areas of the inner city of Byzantium to provide citizens with fresh fruit and vegetables were irrigated by cisterns – open or covered water reservoirs. While open cisterns like the Çukurbostan on Fevzi Paşa Caddesi were constructed in less populous areas, covered cisterns – often the substructures of major buildings such as churches, covered markets or latterly mosques (for instance, the Nuruosmaniye mosque) – were more common in the inner city. Byzantine Constantinople had some 60 covered cisterns.

The Yerebatan Sarayı is one of the most impressive of these ancient engineering structures and the only one still in its original condition. Built by the emperor Justinian at the same time as Haghia Sophia (see page 88) and opposite to it, it was forgotten and then rediscovered in 1545 by Petrus Gyllius, who made a search after discovering that people in the neighbourhood obtained water by lowering buckets through their basement floors. It was Gyllius who gave it its present name of 'Underground Palace'.

Measuring 138 by 65 metres with a capacity of 80,000 cubic metres, the Yerebatan Sarayı was the largest underground water reservoir of Constantinople. The skilful brick vaults are supported on 12 rows of 28 columns – 336 in total – positioned at 4-metre intervals. Most of the 8-metre high shafts are topped by Byzantine capitals. Fragments, or building elements out of fashion at the time of the cistern's construction were used. The highlight is the inverted Medusa's head on one of the column's bases at the far left of the cistern.

ADDRESS 7 Yerebatan Caddesi, Sultanahmet, Eminönü
TRANSPORT tram to Sultanahmet
ACCESS open daily 9.00–18.00 (telephone 0212 522 12 59)

Stamboul

Istanbul Reklam building

İstanbul Reklam Binası

The Istanbul Reklam building is an excellent example of new architecture in keeping with the scale of its surroundings. Located on a corner site, it is designed around the small marble *türbe* of Mahmud Nedim, which remains untouched. The long elevation is fragmented in mass and scale into three sections – the upper ground floor, the main floors with bay windows, and the top floor with balconies resting on the roofs of the bays. The building responds to the height of the *türbe* and to it neighbours.

The detailing of glass, hollow steel sections and precast-concrete units is continued in various forms throughout the exterior. Structural elements are expressed and materials left unfinished.

This is a sculptural brutalist building that nevertheless harmonises with the historic district in which it is located.

ADDRESS 25 Babiali Caddesi/Nuru Osmaniye Caddesi, Eminönü
TRANSPORT tram to Çemberlitaş or Sultanahmet
ACCESS none

Çilingiroğlu & Tunca 1965–9

Çilingiroğlu & Tunca 1965–9

Istanbul High School
İstanbul Erkek Lisesi

Originally built as the headquarters of an institution of European bankers set up to control the economic resources of the bankrupt Ottoman government, the Istanbul High School is still a landmark above Eminönü.

Vallaury and D'Aronco's design combines the Beaux-Arts tradition with elements from local oriental architecture – pointed arches, bay windows, timber grilles, overhanging eaves and monumental entrances. An exotic variation of a traditional *hamam* dome with blue and orange glazed coffers is placed over the main marble staircase. The corridors are lit by skylights, glass blocks in the floor and the fanlights of the high doors.

A teacher at the School of Fine Arts and chief of the imperial architects, Vallaury also designed the highly ornate neo-Renaissance façade of the Ottoman Bank in Galata, the eclectic oriental Imperial College of Military Medicine and the neo-classical Archaeological Museum. For D'Aronco, see Laleli fountain, page 132.

ADDRESS 4 Türk Ocağı Sokak/Türk Ocağı Caddesi, Eminönü
TRANSPORT tram to Çemberlitaş or Gülhane
ACCESS ask the porter

Alexandre Vallaury and Raimondo D'Aronco 1899

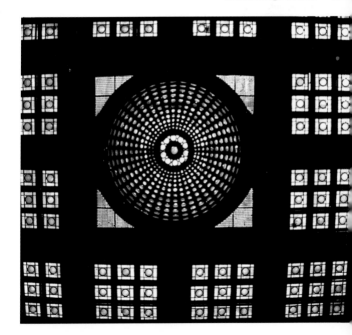

Alexandre Vallaury and Raimondo D'Aronco 1899

Sirkeci station
Sirkeci İstasyonu

Sirkeci station – the terminus of the Orient Express – is a perfect example of the Islamic eclecticism introduced into Istanbul by European architects at the end of the nineteenth century. During the reign of Abdül Hamit II (1876–1909), foreign architects were asked to design several major buildings in the city, mostly new building types for new functions. Jachmund had received a grant from the German government to study the history of Ottoman architecture and was working as a teacher at the Istanbul School of Civil Engineering. Kemalettin Bey (see page 54), one of the leaders of the first national architectural movement, was a student of and later an assistant to Jachmund.

Jachmund's design – with its horseshoe arches, clocktowers and large rose windows – combines neo-classical symmetry, axiality and clarity with an Islamic-style structure. Though his building demonstrates a total lack of awareness of the stylistic differences between various Islamic regions and periods, it was well received and the new eclecticism had a substantial impact on the developing architectural profession.

Sadly, one of the Topkapı palace pavilions had to be demolished to make way for this exercise in pseudo-Islamic architecture.

Stamboul

ADDRESS Sirkeci İstasyon Caddesi, Sirkeci, Eminönü
TRANSPORT bus to Eminönü or tram to Sirkeci

Jachmund 1889

Jachmund 1889

Office building
4 Vakıf Hanı

The 4 Vakıf Hanı is the masterpiece of Kemalettin Bey (see page 54). Located in the busy business district of Bahçekapı, the large seven-storey office block demonstrates the principles of the first national architectural movement, of which Bey was one of the leaders.

The well-ordered, well-proportioned façade is distinguished by its richly coloured tiles and variety of window forms: tall rounded arches over the windows of the ground and mezzanine floors, a different series for the next two floors, triple windows on the two upper floors, and windows divided by columns on the top floor. The strong frames emphasise the horizontal and vertical lines of the façade.

Surprisingly, a steel skeleton lies behind the cut-stone façade, while the corner towers with their onion domes are purely decorative. The impressive interior with its lofty central courtyard and galleries is well worth seeing.

Also look at Liman Hanı, 11 Yalı Köşkü Caddesi.

ADDRESS 64–8 Hamidiye Caddesi, Bahçekapı, Eminönü
TRANSPORT bus to Eminönü or tram to Sirkeci
ACCESS open

Stamboul

Kemalettin Bey 1912–26

Kemalettin Bey 1912–26

Flora Han

The turn of the century was a time of architectural eclecticism in European cities, and Istanbul was no exception. Art nouveau arrived here between 1898 and 1900 and had two phases of popularity – between 1900 and 1915 and 1922 and 1930.

The Flora Han is appropriately named: its façades are extensively decorated with roses. The rose motif appears in friezes, on the upper levels of the vertical strip of the façade and as a single element defining the windows. And the curved balconies on both sides of the five-storey corner building have art nouveau iron railings.

The building is now used as offices, with shops on the ground floor. Although in bad condition, it make its presence felt in an area dominated by Ottoman revivalism.

For other examples of art nouveau, visit the area around İstiklal Caddesi (the former Grand rue de Pera, see page 140). Especially noteworthy are 403 İstiklal Caddesi, the Pina apartments on Asmalı Mescit Sokağı, Kont Otel on Mis Sokağı, 30 Büyük Parmakkapı Sokağı and 7 Sofyalı Sokağı. Also see Raimondo D'Aronco's projects (pages 132 and 146).

ADDRESS 18 Şehinşah Pehlevi Caddesi, Sirkeci, Eminönü
TRANSPORT bus to Eminönü
ACCESS shops open, ask permission for offices

Stamboul

Central Post Office
Büyük Postahane

The Central Post Office was the first and major work of Vedat Tek (1873–1942). Vedat studied painting, civil engineering and architecture in Paris before returning to Istanbul, where he worked for the municipality and taught at the School of Fine Arts. Together with Kemalettin Bey (see page 54), he was one of the founders of the first national architectural movement, in which architects tried to combine elements from their Ottoman heritage with western technology to produce a contemporary national architecture that would harmonise with its historical surroundings. This was the equivalent of eclectic historicism elsewhere in Europe.

Vedat's design for the post office uses Ottoman architectural elements such as pointed arches and traditional-style tiles, designed by the architect himself. The huge mass of the façade is symmetrically composed, with overhanging eaves and pilasters with Corinthian capitals. The 15-metre-high glazed court, probably inspired by the large atriums popular in nineteenth-century banks, is designed to introduce as much light as possible into the interior. The building is attached to a small mosque at the rear.

ADDRESS Şehinşah Pehlevi Caddesi, Cağaloğlu, Eminönü
TRANSPORT bus to Eminönü or tram to Sirkeci
ACCESS open

Vedat Tek 1909

Stamboul

Vedat Tek 1909

German Oriental Bank
Germanya Hanı

The late nineteenth century was a time of strong competition between France and Germany for economic and cultural dominance in Istanbul. The School of Fine Arts, modelled on the Ecole Nationale des Beaux-Arts in Paris, was opened in 1882, and the German-influenced School of Civil Engineering followed in 1884.

Like other German buildings of this period such as the German embassy, the large neo-Renaissance grey stone mass of the German Oriental Bank with its huge tower and copper dome is located in a prominent position and is clearly visible from a distance. Unlike the Sirkeci station (see page 106), where Jachmund tried to design a building that would harmonise with its environment, the bank is in a ponderous central-European style that would have been in stark contrast with the well-proportioned timber houses that dominated the neighbourhood at the time. An unusual feature is the interpretation of the rounded corner: the four-storey main elevation carries fluting as though it were an enormous, flat column and is surmounted by a temple which forms the top of the corner tower.

A restoration was carried out in 1992 by M Sinan Genim.

ADDRESS Vakıf Hanı Sokak/Şeyhülislam Hayri Efendi Caddesi, Bahçekapı, Eminönü
TRANSPORT bus to Eminönü or tram to Sirkeci
ACCESS open

Jachmund

Jachmund

Mehmet Efendi coffee shop
Kurukahveci Mehmet Efendi Mahdumları

The first wave of international style architecture appeared in Turkey between 1929 and the outbreak of the Second World War, fuelled by the need to establish Ankara as the new capital of the Republic and by the numerous foreign architects working in Turkey at the time. But whereas Ankara embraced a more homogenous modernism in its quest to renew itself as a major international centre, Istanbul remained more eclectic, with many of its modern buildings including elements of Ottoman revivalism and art deco.

The jewel-like Mehmet Efendi coffee shop is easy to miss in the crowded streets behind the Egyptian Bazaar. It is an attractive mixture of modern structure, art deco details and modified Ottoman elements such as the large overhanging eaves above the ground floor. It has sophisticated proportions and a balanced relationship between open and closed areas and sculptural and flat elements.

The ground floor is transparent, a skeleton of columns and beams. The overhanging eaves separate this open floor from the more closed upper storey with its horizontal window element running around the corner. Note the details – the steel grille in front of the window, the pipes and guttering, the graphics and the art deco staircase inside. And, of course, the delicious coffee.

Other art deco buildings worth seeing include apartment buildings such as the Bosfor and Ankara Palas in İnönü Caddesi, Gümüşsuyu, and the Mehmet Efendi coffee shop in Söğütlüçeşme Caddesi, Kadıköy.

ADDRESS Kalcın Sokak/Tahmis Caddesi, Eminönü
TRANSPORT bus to Eminönü
ACCESS open

Zühtü 1932

Stamboul

Zühtü 1932

Rüstem Paşa mosque

Rüstem Paşa Camii

The Rüstem Paşa mosque was built by Sinan for the Grand Vezir Rüstem Paşa four years after the Süleymaniye and a decade before the Selimiye in Edirne, for which it was a prototype. Situated below the Süleymaniye in the bustling market of Eminönü, the mosque is raised on a terrace above a collection of shops and workshops to enable it to dominate its surroundings – a common trick when building mosques in densely populated areas.

The courtyard, reached via steps, contains an unusual double porch giving access to the mosque. The main space is rectangular, but the focus is an octagon set to one side of this area to allow for as much uninterrupted space as possible. The dome is supported on massive octagonal piers and flanked by galleries roofed by smaller domes.

The mosque is famous for its tiles, which cover the walls and piers to an extent that only a sultan or grand vezir could afford. The richest of these are the deep red tiles on the *mihrab* wall.

ADDRESS 190–2 Hasırcılar Caddesi, Eminönü
TRANSPORT bus to Eminönü
ACCESS open

Sinan 1561

Sinan 1561

Beyoğlu

Galata bridge
Galata Köprüsü

The first bridge to connect the commercial centre of Galata with the railway and ferry termini of Eminönü in the same place as today's Galata bridge was a 500-metre-long timber structure erected in 1845. In 1863 this was replaced by a larger and sturdier timber toll bridge and in 1877 by an iron structure with wood planking 480 metres long and 14 metres wide supported on 24 pontoons.

In 1909–12 this was superseded by a bridge of similar construction but almost twice as wide erected by the German contractor MAN. This time a rotating central section allowed taller ships to pass and the bridge became famous in international architectural circles following the addition of a suspended level of shops and restaurants. But the pontoons slowed the speed of the Golden Horn current and a new bridge without pontoons was deemed necessary. In the late 1980s, when plans were well under way, the old bridge burnt down. Fragments were reused in a new bridge between Hasköy and Balat.

Like its predecessor, the new Galata bridge combines transport and commerce. Made of steel, it is supported on 114 columns, each 2 metres wide and 80 metres high. The central section can be hoisted up between the four circulation towers on pontoons. The bridge has six traffic lanes and four walkways, two flanking the vehicular lanes and two on each side of the suspended commercial level – still closed at the time of writing – which has an area of 6000 square metres.

Although it could become an interesting, lively urban space, the new bridge lacks the charm and architectural quality of its predecessor.

ADDRESS between Karaköy (Galata) and Eminönü
CONTRACTOR STFA & Thyssen
TRANSPORT bus to Karaköy or Eminönü

Beyoğlu

1990–2

1990–2

Rahmi M Koç industrial museum
Rahmi M Koç Sanayi Müzesi

Harmoniously combining old and new, the Koç museum is a successful attempt to preserve Istanbul's historic building stock by conversion.

Located in the former Jewish quarter of Hasköy, the nineteenth-century building was originally an anchor foundry. Two storeys high with a square floor plan, its walls are of dressed stone with reddish mortar combined with brick courses as tie-beams – a common method of construction for secular buildings in Ottoman times. The roof has five domes, each sitting on a brick cornice.

The new museum is made up of the former anchor foundry, a courtyard above an underground exhibition hall and a café building. The single space of the foundry has been divided into a lower level containing the entrance and the connection to the underground exhibition hall and a two-storey exhibition space with a steel gallery. The original materials and colours of the foundry have been preserved, but the addition is in concrete, steel and glass – an appropriate and striking contrast. A glazed gangway is clearly marked as a new intervention in an old building, but less successful are the new café building and the caretaker's lodge, which try to imitate the original foundry. The open courtyard works convincingly as a recreational area and exhibition space.

Beyoğlu

ADDRESS 27 Hasköy Caddesi, Hasköy, Beyoğlu
TRANSPORT bus 399E, 399H to Hasköy
ACCESS 10.00–17.00 daily except Mondays (telephone 0212 256 71 53)

Garanti Koza 1994

Beyoğlu

Garanti Koza 1994

Sütlüce abattoir
Sütlüce Mezbaharlar

An empty abattoir with an unclear destiny.

This solemn though eclectic industrial complex, its two bright yellow water towers visible from afar, continues to decay while the decision on whether it will become an art museum financed by the private investor Erol Aksoy or part of the Mimar Sinan University (former School of Fine Arts) is debated.

The complex consists of a long main block, its roof pierced by the water towers, running parallel to the Golden Horn, with several halls positioned at right angles to it. Seen from the water, it is a telling example of oriental eclecticism. Its shallow pitched roofs with their overhanging eaves and its pointed arches introduce traditional Ottoman elements into a stuccoed façade whose vertically proportioned window openings – together with the gabled walls – tell of the heritage of its German architect.

Istanbul's main abattoir was moved here from Tophane in 1923, but it was later recognised to introduce too much pollution into the Golden Horn. The main abattoir was therefore moved to Tuzla in 1990 and this one closed in 1992. A jewel from the outside, it still smells of meat.

Beyoğlu

ADDRESS Karaağaç Caddesi, Sütlüce
TRANSPORT bus 399E, 399H to Sütlüce
ACCESS ask the guard

pre-1920

27

Beyoğlu

pre-1920

Aksigorta insurance building
Minerva Han

Until the 1840s the city's significant buildings – palaces, mosques and so on – were concentrated in Stamboul, but by the end of the century a new centre had arisen as the Karaköy area near the harbour and the Galata bridge developed as a business district.

New building types – banks and international trade institutions – were expressed in new architectural styles, predominantly classical revivalism, with a free use of elements from different periods and countries, gothic revivalism, Ottoman revivalism and art nouveau. The new buildings were typically massive stone structures, four or five stories high, with imposing façades and huge interior atriums.

The Minerva Han, built on a sloping corner site and now used by the Aksigorta insurance company, is a fine example of the first national architectural movement, with a combination of traditional Ottoman architectural elements such as overhanging eaves and tiles with European influences such as the sculptures on the façade. It is divided vertically according to classical doctrine: a two-storey base, three-storey central section and single-storey attic. The cornices which define the three parts are reinterpreted as continuous balconies. The curved corner is emphasised by a massive framed entrance, blue-painted window surrounds and the stepping up of the eaves. Placed next to the grilled exterior of the neighbouring İmar Bankası, it adds interest to the corner of Voyvoda Caddesi.

ADDRESS Yüksek Kaldırım Caddesi/Voyvoda Caddesi, Karaköy, Beyoğlu
TRANSPORT bus to Karaköy, Galata Köprüsü
ACCESS ask the porter

Beyoğlu

Sarip Sabancı 1911

Beyoğlu

Sarip Sabancı 1911

Kamondo stairs

Kamondo Merdivenleri

More of an urban sculpture than a circulation route.

With its plastered parapet walls and elliptical plant troughs, the figure of eight of the Kamondo stairs connects Voyvoda Caddesi and the Kamondo Sokağı. A Jewish banker whose family arrived in Istanbul at the end of the eighteenth century, Avram Kamondo was the first foreigner in the Ottoman empire to be allowed to own property. The staircase was restored in 1985.

Buildings of interest in Voyvoda Caddesi include the Osmanlı Bankası by Alexandre Vallaury, the Türkiye İs Bankası at the corner of Tegmen Hüseyin Soku Sokağı, an example of the first national architectural movement, the newly restored Tütünbank and the Nordstern Sigorta building.

Beyoğlu

ADDRESS Voyvoda Caddesi, Karaköy, Beyoğlu
TRANSPORT bus to Karaköy or Tünel to Karaköy
ACCESS open

Laleli fountain
Laleli Çeşme

An unexpected break in the dense urban fabric around the Galata tower, the Laleli fountain stands at the corner of two steep streets.

Italian architect Raimondo D'Aronco (1857–1932) lived in Istanbul from 1893 to 1909, during which time he was highly influential in the development of the city's architecture. Initially he had a preference for eclecticism, designing some buildings with Alexandre Vallaury including the Ottoman revivalist Marmara University in Haydarpaşa and Istanbul High School (see page 104). He was chief of the imperial architects from 1896 to 1908, contributing several buildings to the Yıldız palace (see page 208). After 1900 he moved towards an art nouveau style, which he was first to introduce to Istanbul.

The Laleli fountain is a tiny but impressive example of art nouveau. Based on geometric shapes, it is square in plan with rectangular basins protected by semicircular canopies, the niche for the water spout adorned by a triangular relief. The relationship with D'Aronco's Şeyh Zafir complex (see page 204) is obvious. The fountain is decorated with floral motifs, especially the top, which has carved tendrils and a medallion at the corner.

Noteworthy D'Aronco buildings not published here include the Merzifonlu mosque in Karaköy, the Cemil Bey Yalısı (now a restaurant) in Kireçburnu, the Italian embassy summer residence in Tarabya, the Egyptian embassy in Bebek and the Cumhurbaşkanlığı Yazlık Konutu (prime minister's summer residence) in Yeniköy.

ADDRESS Laleli Çeşme Sokak/Şair Ziya Paşa Caddesi, Galata, Beyoğlu

Raimondo D'Aronco

Raimondo D'Aronco

Galata tower
Galata Kulesi

Although permanently threatened by the rise of neighbouring buildings, the famous tower still stands as Galata's major landmark.

The Galata tower marked the apex of the fortifications built to defend the independence of the Genoese colony of Galata from Constantinople (see Grand rue de Pera, page 140). The best-preserved section of the fortifications, a long narrow rectangle along the Golden Horn, is visible below it. Reinforced in 1446 and damaged several times by earthquakes, storms and fires, the tower survived the demolition of most of the rest of the walls in the mid-nineteenth century. Between 1964 and 1967 it was restored by Köksal Anadol, who returned it to its original silhouette by recreating its conical roof.

Just under 68 metres high, the tower consists of a cylindrical trunk with 3.5-metre-thick walls. The two uppermost levels (the eighth and ninth floors, which house a restaurant and viewing platform) have arched windows. The rest of the tower has very few openings. It contains a small museum, offices and kitchens above a double-height entrance. Concrete groin floors separate the storeys.

In 1989 the municipality of Istanbul launched a project to create a public recreational area around the tower and restore the nearby fortifications and fountain, providing Galata with a much-needed open public space.

ADDRESS Büyük Hendek Sokak/Camekân Sokak/Galata Kulesi Sokak
RECREATIONAL AREA Kemal Akçay (Municipality of Istanbul)
TRANSPORT walk from Karaköy or Tünel
ACCESS museum open 8.00–21.00; restaurant from 21.00

1348–9, restoration Köksal Anadol 1964–7

Beyoğlu

1348–9, restoration Köksal Anadol 1964–7

Cannon house

Tophane

The principal military foundry of the Ottoman empire was established on this site by Mehmet II shortly after the conquest of 1453. It was extended by Beyazit II, then demolished and replaced by Süleyman the Magnificent in preparation for his expansionist campaigns. The present structure, once part of a great complex, was built by Selim III as part of his programme to reform the Ottoman army.

The impressive rectangular building of brick and stone is visible from a distance and has a strong urban presence. Above the massive, almost unbroken base is a finely detailed façade composed of arches filled with small red hexagonal openings. The roof has tall ventilation towers and recessed domes.

The building was partly restored and in 1955 it was to be reopened as part of the Military Museum, but lack of money led to it being used as a museum warehouse. In 1993 the buildings were given to the Mimar Sinan University (former School of Fine Arts) and were designated for use as a centre to support artistic and industrial co-operation between Turkish and French universities. The project is to be realised in two phases: first the preservation and authentic restoration of the original building by Halüh Sezgin, and second the addition of a new building (1770 square metres) by Philippe Robert between the two existing ones.

Also look at Sinan's Molla Çelebi mosque in Fındıklı (1566) and the Koca Yusuf Paşa fountain house (1787).

ADDRESS Necatibey Caddesi/Boğazkesen Caddesi, Tophane, Beyoğlu
TRANSPORT bus from any stop between Taksim and Eminönü to Tophane
ACCESS none

Tophane fountain
Tophane Çeşmesi

The architectural and artistic effort expended on fountains demonstrates the importance of the water supply in the Ottoman city. Every mosque required a *şadırvan* (a fountain for ritual ablutions before prayer, usually positioned in the centre of the courtyard) and many of the mosque complexes included a *sebil* (an enclosed fountain staffed by an attendant who issued cups of water from behind a grille). Public fountains (*çeşmes*) were either modest structures built against the walls of houses or free-standing monuments. Many great baroque fountains were erected between 1728 and 1732, the so-called 'Tulip period'.

The Tophane Çeşmesi, to the north of Sinan's Kılıç Ali Paşa mosque (1580), is one of the most famous of these. A freestanding monument with a domed roof with a timber-coffered soffit and overhanging eaves, it was built by Mahmut I and was the centre of local life. The compact, highly decorated structure has marble walls covered with floral designs and arabesques which were originally painted and gilded. The sides have large arches flanked by tall niches with honeycomb semidomes and the corners are decorated with honeycombs, inscribed plaques and shells.

The most famous *çeşme* is the Ahmet III fountain at the Topkapı gate (Soğuk Çeşme Sokağı) built in 1728 and currently under restoration.

ADDRESS Necatibey Caddesi/Tophane İskele Caddesi, Tophane, Beyoğlu
TRANSPORT bus from any stop between Taksim and Eminönü to Tophane

Beyoğlu

1732

1732

Grand rue de Pera
İstiklal Caddesi (from Tünel to Taksim)

Once lined solely with the impressive mansions of merchants and ambassadors, today the İstiklal Caddesi (formerly the Grand rue de Pera) is the main shopping street and centre of western Istanbul.

Following the end of the Latin occupation of Constantinople in 1261 Galata was granted to the Genoese and given the status of a semi-independent colony. After the Ottoman conquest of 1453 the area became the European quarter of the city, occupied by foreign merchants and ambassadors, Sephardic Jews expelled by the Spanish in 1492, Moorish refugees and Greeks and Armenians. As the Galata area began to become crowded in the seventeenth century, many of the ambassadors and richer merchants moved out to the north, to the hills of Pera, building enormous new mansions along the Grand rue de Pera. The largely immigrant population kept intense contact with its European roots and established European ways of living in the district.

The mid-nineteenth century was a period of intense economic and socio-political transformation of the Ottoman capital and Pera experienced a building boom. But a great fire in 1870 destroyed large parts of the area, by now a densely populated timber-built neighbourhood. Some 3000 buildings were demolished, which led to a law demanding that new buildings be of stone. Soon Galata and Pera were dotted with structures that competed in their dimensions and stylistic aspirations with the Byzantine and Ottoman monuments of Stamboul. Classical revivalism was the most popular style.

The heyday of Pera was the first quarter of the twentieth century; the foundation of the Turkish Republic in 1923 brought a marked rise in nationalism strengthened by post-war policies against non-Muslims which led to the repatriation of many Greek citizens while many Jews left for Israel. The area was subsequently occupied by immigrants from

rural areas and people of low income. Problems in clarifying the ownership of the buildings contributed to their decay. During the following decades gambling, prostitution and illegal businesses spread through Beyoğlu. From the 1960s to the 1980s the İstiklal Caddesi ceded its position as a major shopping street to the Halaskargazi Caddesi in Şişli and others.

By the end of the 1980s a new consciousness of the value of the area, generated mainly by successful young individualists, had regenerated Beyoğlu. The ground floors of more and more buildings were restored, though the upper floors often remained empty. Restaurants, bars, cinemas, bookshops, galleries and small workshops appeared; streetvendors were to be found at every corner.

In the early 1990s the tram was reinstalled and İstiklal Caddesi pedestrianised to create a high-quality urban space of tremendous value in a city suffocating with traffic congestion. But even today the poor condition of the buildings and the wrecked infrastructure (sewage, water supply, electricity) make the area surrounding İstiklal Caddesi unattractive to live in. On the other hand, the combination of thriving commerce and substandard living conditions makes the quarter accessible to poorer citizens who are able to inhabit a centre not a ghetto.

We recommend a stroll through the dense side streets of Pera and neighbouring Cihangir.

Beyoğlu

TRANSPORT Tünel to İstiklal Caddesi, bus to Taksim

Underground funicular railway
Tünel

Linking Karaköy (Galata) and Pera (İstiklal Caddesi), the Istanbul Tünel is allegedly the oldest and shortest underground railway in Europe.

For the sake of economy, the 555-metre-long tunnel had to follow the path of existing roads, coping with a slope of between 2 and 15 per cent and a level difference of 62 metres. The Tünel is 6.7 metres wide and 4.9 metres high. Originally a two-car train ran on each of the two parallel tracks – one for passengers, divided into first and second class with separate compartments for men and women, and the other for merchandise, animals and even horse-drawn carriages.

In 1900 both of the timber terminus buildings were replaced by stone structures. After the formation of the Turkish Republic in 1923 the private company responsible for the railway was nationalised. At the end of the 1960s the old carriages, now in the Tram Museum in Kadıköy, were replaced by the present turquoise boxes, well worth the 80-second journey.

The success of the Tünel led to several other proposals for underground transport. But the city's topography, dense urban structure and lack of financial resources have until recently proved insurmountable barriers. Now a second underground project has started: a metro from Taksim to Etiler. Further projected lines lie in the drawers of the city planning department.

Also look at the nearby Mevlevihanesi (dervish monastery) of 1492 in Galip Dede Caddesi.

ADDRESS 2 Tünel Meydanı (Pera) or Tersane Caddesi/Yüzbaşı Sabahattin Evren Caddesi (Karaköy)
COST £250,000 (in 1875)

Beyoğlu

Eugène Henri Gavand 1875

Beyoğlu

Eugène Henri Gavand 1875

Botter house

The Botter house was the first art nouveau building in Pera. Designed for the Dutchman Botter, the chief tailor and couturier to the imperial court of Abdül Hamit II, it seemed appropriate to use the latest fashion in architecture for a fashion showroom. D'Aronco (see Laleli fountain, page 132) was much admired for this extraordinary work.

Erected on a typical deep site with a narrow frontage, the seven-storey building was divided into showrooms and workshops on the ground and first floors with living quarters for the Botter family on the upper levels. An elliptical staircase and elevator link the two sections. To maximise the window area for the ground-floor showroom, the entrance had to be placed asymmetrically; from the first floor upwards, all storeys are symmetrical in plan.

The natural stone façade – a mix of neo-baroque and Vienna secession – has four huge pilasters connected by an elaborate floral frieze above the third floor. This motif is repeated on the entrance gate and turrets. The roof level has a curved balustrade. At first-floor level there is a semi-elliptical balcony with cast-iron railings.

The two business levels with their stained-glass windows looking on to an interior courtyard were the most sophisticated areas. The showroom walls were covered with fabric and mirrors. The building was embellished with art nouveau light fittings both inside and outside.

Unfortunately the interior was destroyed when the building was converted into a bank in 1960. Though it is classified as a historic monument, the present owners do not maintain it adequately.

ADDRESS 475–7 İstiklal Caddesi
TRANSPORT walk from Tünel
ACCESS open at least to see staircase

Beyoğlu

Raimondo D'Aronco 1900

Beyoğlu

Raimondo D'Aronco 1900

Church of St Mary Draperis
Santa Maria Draperis Kilisesi

You could easily miss this church since the street entrance, a gate in the façade of the Santa Maria Han, gives only a hint that there is another building behind. On passing through the gate and *han*, 49 steps lead to the humble church below. The back entrance at 37 Tom-Tom Kaptan Sokak reveals the church's peculiar situation even more clearly: unlike mosques, which were built on prominent hilltop sites, the church is completely integrated into the surrounding topography and dense urban fabric – probably a result of a restriction forbidding non-Muslim buildings to appear on the city's skyline that held sway until the beginning of the nineteenth century.

The first stone church on this site was built in 1769. After its destruction in the 1870 Pera fire it was rebuilt, together with the Santa Maria Han, in 1904. The building consists of a nave with one-and-a-half side aisles and no apse. The interior is an interesting mix of Christian and Islamic elements. For a time the church was used as the Austro-Hungarian embassy.

Other 'hidden' churches in Beyoğlu include the Orthodox church in Danışman Gecidi/Emir Nevruz Sokak; the church of St Mary at 31 Sakızağacı Caddesi; and the Armenian church at 2 Berurkar Cikmazi. For a bolder statement, see the church of St Anthony of Padua at 327 İstiklal Caddesi, one of the largest Roman Catholic sanctuaries in the city.

ADDRESS 425–35 İstiklal Caddesi
TRANSPORT walk from Tünel
ACCESS open

Beyoğlu

Guglielmo Semprini 1904

Beyoğlu

Guglielmo Semprini 1904

Çukurcuma baths
Çukurcuma Hamamı

The *hamam* serves a functional purpose, is a social occasion and is part of Islamic ritual.

*Hamam*s, always built as part of a pious foundation or mosque complex, come in two types: public baths, equipped only with running water in accordance with the Muslim belief that only running water is cleansing, and thermal baths, which include a swimming pool or basin, as at the Yalova Termal outside Istanbul. The *hamam* consists of three main rooms: a large anteroom (*camekân*) used for changing, relaxing and socialising; a cool room (*soğukluk*) which acts as a buffer zone of intermediate temperature; and a steam room (*sıcaklık* or *hararet*) containing basins with running warm and cold water and a central raised marble slab (*göbektaşı*) for massages. There is also a furnace room, toilets and sometimes rooms for depilation. The sexes are separated, so there is either a single set of rooms for use by men and women at different times or a double set of rooms, one for each sex.

*Hamam*s are functional buildings of modest dimensions. They are usually made up of a series of cubic spaces surmounted by domes lit by bull's-eye skylights. Because they are entirely inward-looking with no need for views or outside light, their plan can easily be organised to suit the shape and orientation of the site. Single *hamam*s are often long, linear buildings; the two sets of rooms in double *hamam*s usually run parallel to each other or interlock, though in one case at least they are placed end to end (see Baths of Roxelana, page 84).

We have chosen the Çukurcuma baths to illustrate the single *hamam* – first because of its extraordinary sloping site and second because a visit requires an exploration of the mysterious side streets of the Cihangir neighbourhood. This area was supplied with water following a donation by the valide sultan (the mother of Mahmut II) in 1831 and was soon

after 1831

after 1831

furnished with a number of baths and fountains. The Çukurcuma is an ordinary *hamam*, decayed and dirty but light and friendly.

The street façade is in stark contrast with the first space the visitor encounters – the inward-looking cubic *camekân*, lit by a shallow clerestory. This high space has a gallery giving access to small cells for massages and relaxation. There is also a rear entrance on Bostanbaşı Caddesi.

Also worth a visit is the Ağa Hamamı, 64 Turnacıbaşı Sokak, and the Galatasaray Hamamı, 24 Turnacıbaşı Sokak.

Beyoğlu

ADDRESS 57 Çukurcuma Caddesi
TRANSPORT walk from İstiklal Caddesi
ACCESS open (telephone 0212 243 24 01)

after 1831

after 1831

Mudo shop

The carefully detailed façade of this five-storey building is decorated in art nouveau style. The shop at ground level – a double-height space partially divided into two levels by a gallery – carries the same ornamental details inside, its walls entirely covered with wooden panels and glass cases. If you disregard the designer goods and the shiny new finish of the restored furnishings, you could easily imagine yourself in the 1920s.

Also worth looking at is the Markiz Pastanesi café at 362 İstiklal Caddesi, near Asmali Mescit Sokak, unfortunately now empty.

ADDRESS 401–3 İstiklal Caddesi
CONTRACTORS G & A Michelini
TRANSPORT walk from Tünel
ACCESS open

A D Yenidunia & C P Kyriakides 1920

Pera Palas hotel

An increase in trade with Europe in the second half of the nineteenth century led to a demand for European-style hotels in Istanbul. Built for the Compagnie Internationale des Wagons-lits et des Grands Expresses Européens, the Pera Palas was at the turn of the century the largest hotel in Pera. Renowned for its many balls, it numbered among its guests Greta Garbo, Mata Hari and Agatha Christie, who wrote the thriller *Murder on the Orient Express* here. Atatürk's room (no. 101) is now preserved as a museum piece. Also from the same period is the more modest Hotel Bristol at 235 Meşrutiyet Caddesi.

Constructed on a 26 by 48-metre base, the cubic Pera Palas consists of two basement levels, a ground floor, five upper storeys and a roof level. From the outside it has the appearance of a severe and massive block, though its four classicist elevations are given individuality and rhythm by the play of pilasters, ionic columns, balconies and window openings of different shapes and sizes. The stone-clad corners frame and separate the façades while the continuous cornice unites them.

On entering the lofty reception area, the visitor gets a first glimpse of the elaborate interior. The heart of the building is the ballroom on the upper ground floor, conceived as a two-storey courtyard roofed by six turquoise domes. Windows run around the upper level, lighting the bedroom corridors behind. The decoration is oriental in flavour and the furniture – for instance the damask tables with mother-of-pearl inlays – is strikingly original.

To the west are three dining rooms – one large and two small – with views of the Golden Horn, particularly beautiful at sunset. Also worth looking at is the wrought-iron art nouveau lift. The café, refurbished after a fire, also has art nouveau decoration.

The atmosphere of the public spaces of the Pera Palas takes the visitor

Beyoğlu

Alexandre Vallaury 1892

Beyoğlu

Alexandre Vallaury 1892

back to the turn of the century, when the Beyoğlu district was in its heyday. But the individual rooms are shabby and fail to justify the exorbitant prices charged.

The busy street to the west (Tarlabaşı) was constructed in the early 1980s to connect the Golden Horn and Taksim. Requiring the sacrifice of a historic area for its realisation, it is typical of the planning nightmares of Istanbul's recent history.

ADDRESS 98–100 Meşrutiyet Caddesi, Tepebaşı, Beyoğlu
TRANSPORT bus to Tepebaşı or walk from İstiklal Caddesi
ACCESS open

Beyoğlu

Alexandre Vallaury 1892

Alexandre Vallaury 1892

Robinson Crusoe bookshop
Robinson Crusoe Kitabevi

Books, nothing but books! The restriction of a low budget was turned to advantage by allowing the goods themselves to become the major element in the design of the interior.

The shop is located in one of the gatehouses of the nineteenth-century Dutch embassy. The façade at ground level has been largely replaced by a timber-framed opening that reduces the distinction between inside and outside. The integrated timber sign is the only closed surface. The subdivision of the shop window picks up on the proportions of the first-floor neo-classical façade. Outside opening hours the window can be covered by a traditional-style Ottoman grille.

The interior benefits from the use of few materials and elements. A gallery has been inserted and books are sold on the ground floor and mezzanine with the upper floor used for storage and an office. The steel shelves reach from the timber floor to the vaulted brick ceiling, as if the upper level was supported on walls of books. The shelves can be angled to display magazines or fixed horizontally for books.

Han Tümertekin also designed the Taksim Sanat Galerisi (Taksim art gallery), Cumhuriyet Caddesi, Taksim, Beyoğlu.

Beyoğlu

ADDRESS 389 İstiklal Caddesi
TRANSPORT walk from Tünel
ACCESS open Monday to Saturday 9.30–21.30; Sunday 10.00–21.30

Han Tümertekin 1994

Beyoğlu

Han Tümertekin 1994

Narmanlı Han
(former Russian embassy)

The embassies that line the İstiklal Caddesi played a crucial role in defining the image of nineteenth-century Beyoğlu. Using various historical styles, they competed with each other in monumentality. The French embassy, rebuilt in 1838 in Empire style; the neo-Renaissance British embassy, designed in 1845 by Sir Charles Barry, architect of the Houses of Parliament in London; and the Russian (1838) and Dutch (1855) embassies by the Swiss Fossati brothers are among the outstanding examples. The mix of embassy buildings placed well back from the street and cut off from their neighbours by large gardens and the dense mesh of streetside retail outlets gives the former Grand rue de Pera a unique rhythm.

The Narmanlı Han served as the Russian embassy until the 1840s. Afterwards it was converted into artists' ateliers and writers' lodgings and it now houses workshops, shops and offices. The *han* suffers from an unfortunate mismatch of plan and elevation, street side and court side. The building with symmetrical side wings is arranged around a closed courtyard. But the front elevation gives no hint of this. The curved southern corner and balcony, where one might expect the entrance to be located with the façade treatment continuing around the corner to the west, instead merely disturbs the neo-classical façade. And the entrance itself is a classical symmetrical affair framed by doric pilasters carrying an architrave, frieze and cornice.

An interesting mannerist mixture, in its present state of decay it is a paradise only for cats.

ADDRESS 390 İstiklal Caddesi
TRANSPORT walk from Tünel
ACCESS open

Beyoğlu

before 1838

before 1838

Aynalı arcade
Aynalı Pasajı

The second half of the nineteenth century saw the opening of several department stores and shopping arcades in Istanbul, variations on their European precursors as well as on the Ottoman bazaar (see Covered bazaar, page 74).

Also known as Passage d'Europe, the Aynalı Pasajı, with an area of 1500 square metres, runs parallel to İstiklal Caddesi between two side streets. Its name, 'arcade of mirrors', derives from its interior, where mirrors between the shopfronts enhance the structural transparency.

The neo-classical three-storey building is of brick construction disguised with stone cladding. The first-floor façade has a rhythm of two arched windows with an ornamental central column alternating with niches holding statues on pedestals. Each of the 22 statues represents a craft. The cornice above the first floor is also the second-floor sill.

The arcade, which had fallen into disrepair and was closed, was renovated in 1992–3 at a cost of $600,000. The present building is the result of a sensitive and successful restoration. There are 25 different-sized shops with storage space in the basement. The smaller shops are double height. Two of the shops are connected to the upper floor by internal stairs; the others have office space above, accessible via central staircases at each side of the arcade.

The second floor, covered by a transparent barrel-vault roof, consists of two galleries running the length of the arcade connected by a bridge with a small terrace at each end. Originally used for storage, the space is now about to become a pleasant café.

ADDRESS between Meşrutiyet Caddesi and Sahne Sokak
TRANSPORT walk from Taksim or Tünel
ACCESS open

Beyoğlu

restoration Haluk Sezgin 1992–3

Cité de Pera building

The Cité de Pera building was conceived as a combination of shopping arcade and apartment block – a common building type in nineteenth-century Europe, when an internal shopping street was often integrated into a multi-storey complex. This building, on a 4500-square-metre site and decorated in Second Empire style, became a prototype for apartment schemes in Pera.

The richly ornamented façade is defined by three projecting gables, two with bay windows, and a curved corner and balcony (see Narmanlı Han, page 162). The ground floor with its mezzanine level has arched windows. The L-shaped four-storey Çiçek (flower) arcade has a glazed vaulted roof with a dome at the junction of the two wings. It is decorated internally with pilasters and friezes, with french windows and balconies below the dome, but is still more modest that the building's street façade.

In 1978 the decayed structure of the Cité de Pera building collapsed. Rebuilt in 1988, it now houses 18 residential and office units as well as 24 shops and catering facilities. The restaurants are reached via the arcade, which though neglected is impressive thanks to its volume and plan.

Beyoğlu

ADDRESS İstiklal Caddesi/Sahne Sokak, opposite Galatasaray Lisesi
TRANSPORT walk from Tünel or Taksim
ACCESS open

Cleanthe Zanno 1874–6

Cleanthe Zanno 1874–6

Şemsi building

Strolling along İstiklal Caddesi, one comes across a few buildings that are recognisably influenced by the international style but cast a distinctly oriental spell.

One such is the Şemsi. An example of Turkish modernism, its symmetrical geometric façade mixes international-style components such as horizontal windows with Ottoman elements like window grilles, here transformed into decorative horizontal bars to give a sculptural effect to the otherwise flat façade. The six-storey building, probably dating from the 1960s, has suffered alterations which confuse the composition including a roof addition, a change to the central opening and the removal of some of the bars.

It is said that the architect later became an actor; now his building is a stage for the display of bridal gowns.

ADDRESS 272–4 İstiklal Caddesi
TRANSPORT walk from Taksim
ACCESS shops are open

Beyoğlu

Ercüment Tarcan

Ercüment Tarcan

Anadolu Pasajı and Atlas Çarşısı

An arcade is typically a covered pedestrian passageway flanked by small shops connecting two streets. The standard European arcade, imported into Istanbul in the late nineteenth century, has its roots in the oriental bazaar; Pera spawned another variation that is a combination of the *han* (see Büyük Yeni inn, page 76) and the arcade, not necessarily connecting two streets but with a main entrance on İstiklal Caddesi and sometimes an insignificant back entrance.

Many of Beyoğlu's arcades are in bad condition. Their names – Aznavur Pasajı, Alkazar, Cité de Syrie – tell of the flavour of nineteenth-century Pera. The Anadolu Pasajı and the Atlas Çarşısı are typical, their symmetrical front façades decorated with neo-classical elements that tell of the aspirations of turn-of-the-century Pera.

The early-twentieth-century Anadolu Pasajı is a five-storey *han* on a narrow rectangular site. The skeletal façade is structured by balustrades, pilasters, friezes and french windows giving on to small balconies. Above the entrance is a three-storey bay. The Atlas Çarşısı has a huge first-floor cinema showing foreign films with Turkish subtitles with a pleasant foyer – unfortunately redecorated in cheap materials – and a bar.

Beyoğlu

ADDRESS 207–11 İstiklal Caddesi
TRANSPORT walk from Taksim
ACCESS open (Atlas cinema, telephone 0212 243 75 76)

Bird houses
Kuş Evleri

They look like architectural models but their scale is 1:1. These miniature houses are designed for birds. Birds – symbolic messengers from heaven – have an important role in Islamic tradition and bird houses merit the status of an independent building type within Turkish architecture: full-size buildings imaginatively re-interpreted.

'Negative' examples, chiselled into the walls of buildings, as well as 'positive' examples, supported on brackets – like the double bird house on the wall of the Tourist Information Office in Taksim Square – can both be found. Made of brick or carved stone, they are masterpieces of crafts-manship. Mostly two or three storeys high, they have domes and roofs, windows and doors, friezes and pilasters. Often the main design motif is a projecting bay window.

Dating mostly from Ottoman times, bird houses were attached to or carved into all types of buildings – *medreses*, mosques, aqueducts, houses and schools. A very early instance is the one at the Büyükçekmece bridge; other examples can be found at the Yeni mosque in Eminönü and the Yeni Valide mosque in Üsküdar. Unfortunately more recent architecture has often neglected to include bird houses, though a few contemporary examples – see 228 and 423 Bağdat Caddesi on the Asian side of the Bosphorus – do exist.

Also look at Özgayret Apartmanı, 103 İstiklal Caddesi/Büyük Parmakkapı Sokak, a branch of the Chamber of Architecture and a truly international-style scheme.

ADDRESS Tourist Information Office, Taksim Square

Atatürk culture centre

Atatürk Kültür Merkezi

The Taksim area takes its name from the Taksim water tower (1732). The area was a Christian cemetery until 1869 when it was converted into Istanbul's first public park and a square.

Originally planned as an opera house, the Atatürk culture centre stands at the eastern side of the square. With its travertine-clad side elevations and front façade veiled by a grey steel curtain, it appears to be a closed box during the day. But at night a brightly lit space opens up to the square, separated from it only by an elegant steel mesh. This rhythmic grille, a transformation of the traditional Ottoman grille element, is braced by a self-supporting metal-framed glazed façade. Inside are freestanding columns.

The building has a cruciform plan. The largest block, facing the square, is a three-storey volume that houses the foyers, an art gallery and the main auditorium, with a capacity of 1317. This opens on to a main stage with ancilliary stages, orchestra pit, chorus rooms and workshops at the sides. The block at the rear accommodates the 25-metre-square back stage surrounded by facilities such as a cafeteria, kitchen and service rooms.

Although it is one of the few public buildings in Taksim, the closed daytime façade makes no contribution to the public space. Hayati Tabanlioğlu also designed parts of the Atatürk airport.

Beyoğlu

ADDRESS Taksim Square
TRANSPORT bus, *dolmuş* to Taksim
ACCESS for performances

Hayati Tabanlioğlu 1956–77

Beyoğlu

Hayati Tabanlioğlu 1956–77

Tüten apartment house

This stringent, experimental building belongs to the early period of modern Turkish architecture, from 1927 until the start of the Second World War.

The 32-metre-deep, narrow site required an innovative plan solution: a double T-shaped arrangement allows all rooms to benefit from natural light. Living rooms are located at the front and back, with views on to the street or garden. In between is a service core of bathrooms, kitchens, stairs and corridors. Because of the sloping site, the front of the building has six storeys plus roof level and the back three additional basement storeys.

The construction is concrete frame with brick infill. The front façade projects at one side to align with a neighbouring building, while the recessed part aligns with the other. The two are connected by a quarter-cylinder. Horizontal windows and sills supply plasticity. Nautical bull's-eye windows typical of the period are used. The rear façade also mediates between its neighbours, this time using rectangular elements.

Also look at the Üçler apartment house (1935) by Seyfettin N Arkan on İnönü Caddesi/Ayazpaşa Caddesi and the private gallery of the Ayşe ve Ercüment Kalmık Vakfı Binası in Saray Arkası Sokağı, Ayazpaşa, Gümüşsuyu – a restored old building with a new addition and formal garden by Ayşe Orbay.

ADDRESS İnönü Caddesi, opposite Asker Hastanesi, Gümüşsuyu
TRANSPORT bus to Gümüşsuyu or Taksim
ACCESS offices; worth asking

Beyoğlu

Adil Denktaş 1936

Adil Denktaş 1936

Atatürk library
Atatürk Kitaplığı

The library was originally conceived as part of a cultural complex for the Koç Foundation that was to include a museum and exhibition spaces. In adopting a hexagonal plan with hexagonal skylights, Eldem was re-using his own plan for an unbuilt project for a Turkish restaurant in the Istanbul Hilton.

Superimposed on a triangular structural grid, the split-level complex has the main reading room at the top, lit by skylights in the domes and windows with views towards the Bosphorus. The detailing, fittings and choice of materials – wood, concrete and glass – make it a calm and pleasant place to work.

Eldem's trademarks – vertically proportioned windows, tiled panels and a roof with overhanging eaves – are again to be found.

ADDRESS Miralay Şefik Bey Sokak, Gümüşsuyu, Taksim
TRANSPORT bus to Gümüşsuyu
ACCESS open 9.00–19.00

Sedad Hakkı Eldem 1973–5

Sedad Hakkı Eldem 1973–5

Şişli

Maçka art gallery
Maçka Sanat Galerisi

The gallery was converted from a caretaker's flat in the semi-basement of the Eynam Palas apartment block. The first step was to design an interesting entrance – a courtyard with an inviting undulating wall that also serves as an exterior exhibition space. To emphasise the connection between inside and outside, the same material, a 10 x 10-centimetre beige tile, is used for walls and floors throughout. The tiles provide a neutral background for the modern art on display and sometimes inspire the artists to include them in their work. Tensioned translucent sailcloth is used for the ceiling to give the low room a less oppressive feel and to facilitate homogenous lighting.

The foyer of the Eynam Palas is also worth looking at.

ADDRESS 31 Eytam Caddesi, near Maçka Oteli, Maçka, Şişli
TRANSPORT bus to Harbiye or *dolmuş* to Teşvikiye
ACCESS open (telephone 0212 240 80 23)

Mehmet Konuralp 1976

Mehmet Konuralp 1976

Nazif bar and Yekta restaurant
(formerly Vedat Tek's private residence)

Placed on a sloping triangular site in the exclusive district of Nişantaşı, the private residence of architect Vedat Tek's (see Central post office, page 112) is a masterpiece. Reminiscent of an early Frank Lloyd Wright house with its overhanging eaves and deep balconies, it also reflects Ottoman tradition in its use of elements such as bay windows, arched windows and tiles.

The plan responds to the difficult corner site in a way typical of Turkish houses: the ground floor adopts the irregularities of the site while the upper floors use bay windows to create generous rectangular rooms with views outside. Though the four-storey building is constructed of masonry, it takes on the character of a timber-framed house. Exterior and interior are designed in a sensitive way with many interesting details.

The entrance hall is decorated with turquoise tiles and marble; walls are supported on pilasters. The first-floor Nazif bar retains the painted ceilings, sliding windows with timber grilles, built-in cupboards and fireplace of the original. Recently all the walls have been painted blue. The second floor has been converted into an office, though some details have been salvaged.

Also look at the Istanbul Radio House (Radyo Evi) in Cumhuriyet Caddesi in Harbiye by İsmail Utkular, Doğan Erginbaş and Ömer Günay (1945).

ADDRESS Vali Konağı Caddesi/Süleyman Nazif Sokak, Nişantaşı, Şişli
TRANSPORT bus or *dolmuş* to Harbiye
ACCESS bar and restaurant open October to May

Vedat Tek

Şişli

Şişli

Vedat Tek

House of advertising

Reklamevi

For fans of post-modernism.

There is not much deconstructivism or high-tech architecture in Istanbul; judging from architectural competitions, post-modernism is the most popular recent idiom. Two major approaches can be distinguished: buildings that use elements from classical Ottoman architecture and those that draw on a generalised classical antique vocabulary.

The Reklamevi, which belongs to the latter category, won a prize at the first national architecture exhibition in 1988. Situated on a typical narrow, deep site in a dark side street, the building, which houses advertising agency Young & Rubicam, attracts attention. Its striking façade consists of several layers: outermost is a horizontally ordered natural stone façade with tympanum; underneath is a closed plastered layer supported by a single column; the third layer is five storeys of metal-framed glazing standing on a sill; finally there is a concave semi-cylindrical entrance framed by the column and a column fragment.

Inside, an open spiral staircase connects the floors. Office cells are combined with open-plan space, but unfortunately some of the rooms have no exterior view. The standard of construction is remarkably high for Istanbul.

Also look at the Erkmen-Evi in Cihangir Caddesi and the Koleksiyon Mobilya in Büyükdere, both by the same architect.

ADDRESS 20 Süleyman Nazif Sokak, Teşvikiye, Şişli
TRANSPORT bus to Harbiye or *dolmuş* to Teşvikiye
ACCESS with permission only (telephone 0212 241 35 60)

Şişli

Haydar Karabey 1988

Haydar Karabey 1988

Brav boutique

Brav Butik

Teşvikiye is an area where a number of modern cafés and bars have sprung up and where you can buy European *haute couture* alongside extraordinary Turkish designs.

The Brav boutique is located on the ground floor of an existing building. The new entrance acts as a display case for the designer clothes on sale and as a transitional space between the street and the inside of the shop, 1.6 metres below street level. A staircase guides visitors from the pavement, via a sunken half level to the entrance and then the centre of the shop. The clothes hang on curved steel rails or lie on glass shelves set into the wall, leaving large areas of free space for customers to parade in the garments they are trying on. The fittings are designed to save space, not to be decorative. Materials are left in their natural colours and the restrained details allow the clothes to speak for themselves.

Also look at the Teşvikiye Palas apartment building in Teşvikiye Caddesi.

ADDRESS Velibey Apartment, 5 Bostan Sokak (near Teşvikiye Caddesi), Teşvikiye, Şişli
TRANSPORT bus to Maçka Oteli or *dolmuş* to Teşvikiye
ACCESS open (telephone 0212 261 21 17)

Kerem Erginoğlu & Hasan Çalışlar 1994

Kerem Erginoğlu & Hasan Çalışlar 1994

Beşiktaş

Şark restaurant
Şark Restoranı

With its cruciform plan with a central hall (*sofa*) containing a fountain, overhanging eaves and window treatment, the former Taşlık coffee house was almost a replica of the seventeenth-century Köprülü mansion (see page 244). A controversial building, it stood midway between slavish historicism and a demonstration of the potential of an intelligent contemporary use of historical forms as favoured by the second national architectural movement of the 1940s.

Originally part of a public park and commanding a wonderful view of the Bosphorus, the coffee house was demolished and rebuilt as part of the huge Swiss Hotel complex. Although the new version adopted the original's reinforced-concrete structural frame and extensive use of wood for both exterior and interior, the proportions and scale were changed along with details such as the replacement of the wooden brackets supporting the front bay with concrete ones. Unfortunately Eldem's addition of a fourth wing to the *sofa*, containing the entrance and services, was changed for the new version.

But probably the greatest loss is the surrounding environment – instead of being a small structure on the edge of a beautiful park, the coffee-shop building is squeezed up against an overscaled complex with no consideration of their relationship.

Now a restaurant, it is still worth a visit.

Beşiktaş

ADDRESS Bayıldım Caddesi, Maçka, Beşiktaş
TRANSPORT bus to Dolmabahçe or Maçka
ACCESS open daily except Tuesdays from 19.00
(telephone 0212 259 01 01)

Sedad Hakkı Eldem 1947–8

Beşiktaş

Sedad Hakkı Eldem 1947–8

Dolmabahçe palace

Dolmabahçe Sarayı

The Dolmabahçe palace combines monumental European palace architecture with a traditional Ottoman concept of interior space. Though it lacks the architectural intensity of the Topkapı palace (see page 92), it is a good example of the changes taking place in Istanbul's architecture in the nineteenth century. The first Turkish national assembly took place in the palace in 1877 and Atatürk lived there during his visits to Istanbul.

The nine architects of the Balyan family were for nearly a century the most important and influential architects in Istanbul. Serving under six sultans, they were collectively responsible for the westernisation of the city's architecture. Of Armenian origin, Bali Kalfa Balyan was brought to Istanbul from Kayseri in middle Anatolia when he was a boy. His son Kirkor was chief of the imperial architects under Mahmut 11 (1808–39) and was responsible for the Nusretiye mosque (1822–6) among other works. Though the elder architects of the family got their knowledge of European architecture from drawings and etchings introduced by European travellers and diplomats, Kirkor's son Garabed sent his sons Nikoğos and Sarkis to study at the Ecole des Beaux-Arts in Paris. At first they assisted their father and then became independent architects in their own right.

The Dolmabahçe palace, well tucked into the Bosphorus shoreline, is constructed on a former harbour filled in in the early seventeenth century by Ahmet 1 and his son Osman 11 to extend a royal garden laid out by Mehmet 11 shortly after the conquest. It is this that gives the palace its name (*dolmabahçe* means 'filled-in garden'). The present palace was commissioned by Abdül Mecit 1 and served as the imperial residence of the Ottoman sultans for most of the rest of their rule.

The palace has no sea walls and no mosque (the Dolmabahçe mosque of 1852–3 by Garabed Balyan is outside the palace area). The pavilion

Garabed and Nikoğos Balyan 1846–56

Beşiktaş

Garabed and Nikoğos Balyan 1846–56

arrangement of the traditional Ottoman imperial residence is rejected and views outside are not celebrated. The 'Euro-palace' exterior combines classicist temple-style façades with Italian Renaissance elements and neo-baroque decoration. The eclectic 284-metre façade facing the water explodes the subtle scale of the neighbouring mansions. The other elevations are more modest, except for the richly ornamented baroque gates.

The extensive palace – 285 rooms in all – has a raised middle section containing the throne room and main staircase flanked by wings housing the state rooms, royal apartments and *harem*. The rooms are arranged according to the traditional Ottoman cruciform plan, as in the Çinili Köşkü (see Topkapı palace). The designer of the interiors of Charles Garnier's Paris opera, Sechan, was responsible for interiors of the palace and European furniture like that found in French palaces and mansions was used – an unusual departure for Ottoman architecture.

Beşiktaş

ADDRESS Dolmabahçe Caddesi
TRANSPORT bus to Akaretler
ACCESS open 9.00–15.00, closed
on Mondays and Thursdays

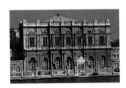

Garabed and Nikoğos Balyan 1846–56

Garabed and Nikoğos Balyan 1846–56

Terraced houses
Akaretler

A statistic from 1882 shows the seriousness of the housing shortage in Istanbul: 26 per cent of the capital's population was homeless. Organised residential developments in the form of terraced houses in modest neighbourhoods were introduced during the second half of the nineteenth century to create moderate-income housing for merchants, bureaucrats, tradesmen and artisans – the only examples of multi-unit dwelling from the Ottoman period.

The Akaretler scheme, built by Sultan Abdül Aziz (1861–76) for the staff of the Dolmabahçe palace, is exceptional in its scale and stylistic significance. Based on western models, the large units have simple symmetrical façades combining western components with traditional local elements such as bay windows. The 90 blocks containing 271 flats line two streets.

Years ago a hotel chain tried to convert the social housing into hotels. People were evicted from their homes but the project was never realised. Then in 1990 the city of Istanbul became the owner and leased the blocks for 49 years to the Yapı Net Holding company. Now the units are to be rented out as offices and private homes – starting with the renovated no. 97 as a showhouse, the spaces are to be restored one by one as soon as tenants are found.

The rear elevations are also worth looking at.

ADDRESS Spor Caddesi, Beşiktaş
RENOVATION Ahmet Duran (Yapı Net Holding)
TRANSPORT bus to Akaretler or *dolmuş* from Taksim
ACCESS open access to the showhouse

Beşiktas

Balyan family 1870

Balyan family 1870

Beşiktaş landing stage
Beşiktaş İskelesi

One of several landing stages designed by Ali Talat (1869–1922), the Beşiktaş İskelesi consists of a two-storey main building with two two-storey buildings set at right angles framing an entrance court. Windows with pointed arches and yellow, red and blue glass, octagonal bay windows with overhanging eaves, corner towers and the symmetrical composition demonstrate the principles of the first national architectural movement.

The plan and functions of the spaces have changed over the years. The present first-floor café with its balcony looking out to the water was a ballroom until 1950. The side buildings, which now contain administration and ticket-sale areas, previously housed a bank and a confectionery shop.

In the nearby park can be found one of Sinan's earliest works, the simple octagonal *türbe* of Süleyman's admiral Barbarossa (Hayrettin Paşa) dating from 1542; a 1940s statue in memory of Barbarossa facing the *türbe*; and Sinan's Sinan Paşa mosque (1555–6). Downstream from the landing stage is the Maritime Museum (Deniz Müzesi).

Beşiktaş

ADDRESS Beşiktaş Caddesi and Barbaros Hayrettin Caddesi, Beşiktaş
TRANSPORT bus or *dolmuş* to Beşiktaş
ACCESS open

Ali Talat 1913

Ali Talat 1913

Yumurcak cinema
Yumurcak Sineması

Rumoured to have been designed by Vedat Tek's son, this cinema is something of a mystery, even among architectural professionals. Located in the busy main shopping street of Beşiktaş, it is easy to miss it if you are not looking upwards. Using a combination of art deco and modern elements, it resembles a 1950s radio.

The three-storey building has projecting upper floors covered by a slightly sloped saddleback. The plastered façade has horizontal windows and vertical pilasters culminating in small turrets. Although the composition at first appears symmetrical, the bull's eye which lights the staircase is not repeated on the right-hand side.

On the street side of the near-rectangular plan there are three shops and the cinema entrance on the ground floor, a tailor's workshop with a side entrance on the first level and technical and service rooms for the cinema on the second floor. The middle part contains the cinema foyer with the dress circle above. The auditorium with its little stage is at the rear.

The Yumurcak is not open as a cinema at present and is only occasionally used for other events. Unfortunately the interior was redecorated in the 1970s.

The apartment building with expressionist curved balconies to the left of the cinema is worth a glance.

ADDRESS Ortabahçe Caddesi, Beşiktaş
TRANSPORT bus to Beşiktaş
ACCESS for special events only (telephone 0212 261 01 91)

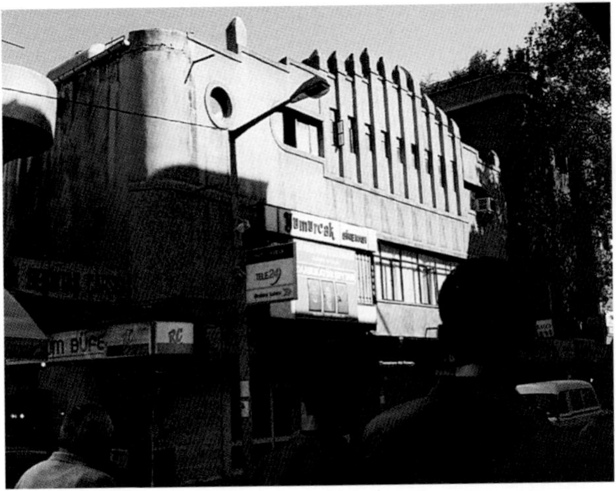
Yumurcak

Şeyh Zafir complex
Şeyh Zafir Türbesi Kitaplığı ve Çeşmesi

This beautiful little complex belongs somewhere between Ottoman architecture and art nouveau. It consists of a central *türbe* (mausoleum) with an adjoining *kitaplık* (library) on one side and a freestanding *çeşme* (fountain) on the other.

Sultan Abdül Hamit II commissioned chief of the imperial architects Raimondo D'Aronco (see page 132) to design the ensemble in honour of the Islamic leader Şeyh Muhammet Zafir in the year of the latter's death. It was D'Aronco's first religious commission and drew on a knowledge of Ottoman architecture amassed from restoring religious buildings destroyed by the 1894 earthquake. If a prototype were required, the nearby *türbe* for Barbarossa (Hayrettin Paşa) by Sinan (1542) could have provided a perfect example.

Measuring 8.5 by 8.5 metres, D'Aronco's *türbe* is based on the Ottoman square plan and is covered by a classical onion-shaped dome. Inside, the transition from cube to dome is resolved through traditional vaulted niches at the residual triangular corners.

The exterior is characterised by its geometric forms and art nouveau decoration. Three of the façades are almost identical; the fourth, oriented towards the Ertuğul Tekke mosque, differs. The semi-circular canopies above vertical windows are reminiscent of the entrance to Otto Wagner's Viennese Karlsplatz station (1899–1900).

The mausoleum is decorated with plant motifs, especially olive branches, with triangular ornamentation on each side of the windows ending at corner turrets. The dome gives the impression of being suspended between these turrets. A horizontal strip of square windows and ornamental shields defines the base of the building. Here a similarity to the work of Frank Lloyd Wright can be seen.

A library is not traditionally part of the brief for a mausoleum complex.

Beşiktaş

Raimondo D'Aronco 1903

Raimondo D'Aronco 1903

Like the *türbe*, this one is square in plan, but is covered by a projecting structure that is half roof and half dome, again flanked by corner turrets. Inside, niches with bookcases frame the Charles Rennie Macintosh-like windows.

The fountain consists of four stepped-back stone blocks with a niche for the water spout and two turrets on top. It is decorated with geometric elements such as triangles and squares as well as the usual inscriptions.

The complex is the result of a long-term encounter between two cultures: an Islamic mausoleum designed with a foreigner's eye.

Beşiktaş

ADDRESS Yıldız Caddesi, Beşiktaş
TRANSPORT bus to Barbaros Bulvarı
ACCESS under reconstruction

Raimondo D'Aronco 1903

Raimondo D'Aronco 1903

Yıldız park

Yıldız Parkı

Istanbul today has too few public green spaces. In the inner city, only Maçka Demokrasi park, Taksim park, Gülhane park (formerly part of the grounds of the Topkapı palace), Yıldız park and the shores of the Golden Horn offer open recreational areas.

Yıldız park, the gardens of the Yıldız palace, was designed by the Frenchman G Le Roi in the nineteenth century, but is based on English park landscaping principles. With an area of 160 hectares, it is by far the largest palace garden in Istanbul. It was connected to the Çırağan palace by a footbridge, originally to allow the women of the palace *harem* to enter the gardens without having to use the public road.

The Yıldız complex is the last sultan's palace built in Istanbul. Although most of its buildings date from the time of Abdül Hamit II (1876–1909), who lived here during his reign, it does not follow the monumental style of the nineteenth-century Dolmabahçe (see page 194) or Çırağan (see page 212) palaces, but consists of individual pavilions like the older Topkapı palace (see page 92).

From outside the park, only the high walls and monumental entrances suggest the presence of an imperial residence. The autonomous pavilions, distributed freely within, are not visible and have no presence in the city – indeed, the conglomeration of eclectic pavilions (arsenal, theatre, library, workshops, guest houses, administrative and residential buildings) creates a city within the city. This conforms with the sultan's desire for isolation and privacy; unlike the Topkapı palace, which was also an administrative centre and seat of government, the function of the Yıldız palace was almost exclusively residential.

Most of the pavilions were designed by Sarkis and Simon Balyan, though Raimondo D'Aronco was responsible for the theatre, porcelain factory and a greenhouse. The Şale Köşkü of 1875, a guest house

Beşiktas

G Le Roi, Sarkis and Simon Balyan, Raimondo D'Aronco et al

Beşiktas

G Le Roi, Sarkis and Simon Balyan, Raimondo D'Aronco et al

modelled on a Swiss chalet, was a collaboration between Sarkis Balyan and D'Aronco.

No other palace has suffered more alterations than Yıldız. The park was redesigned in 1980. The Turkish Touring and Automobile Society (see Istanbul library, page 98) restored some of the buildings including the neo-classical Malta Köşkü in the outer palace garden, the Çadır Köşkü, and a pink and green greenhouse.

Today the various pavilions accommodate the Stagecraft Museum (Sahne Sanatlar Müzesi), the Municipality Museum (Belediye Şehir Müzesi), cafés and other functions.

ADDRESS İlhamur Yıldız Caddesi or Çırağan Caddesi
TRANSPORT bus to Yıldız Üniversitesi or Yıldız Parkı
ACCESS open; Şale Köskü 9.30–17.00 except Mondays and Thursdays (telephone 0212 161 20 43)

Beşiktas

G Le Roi, Sarkis and Simon Balyan, Raimondo D'Aronco et al

G Le Roi, Sarkis and Simon Balyan, Raimondo D'Aronco et al

Çırağan Sarayı hotel
(former Palace of Çırağan)

The Palace of Çırağan was the most sophisticated of the nineteenth-century imperial residences. Built on the site of some old timber mansions, it consisted of ten buildings with a water frontage of 1300 metres. Because it was made up of a series of freestanding pavilions with a unified façade treatment, it was more in keeping with the scale of the surrounding mansions than the Dolmabahçe palace (see page 194) and was a worthwhile addition to the waterfront.

The architects combined European-influenced neo-classicism with Ottoman elements and gave the complex a Moorish feel through such details as the window arches, pilasters with capitals and the cornice. Artists were sent to North Africa and Spain to study important Moorish buildings. The interior was also a combination of Ottoman, Moorish and European elements. The main block consisted of three parts, each with a central hall (*sofa*), as in traditional Turkish houses.

The palace served for three decades as a residence for the deposed Sultan Murat v and his family. From 1909 to 1910 it was the seat of parliament. It burnt down in January 1910 and in the following decades the ruins were used as a football stadium and outdoor swimming pool.

After a restoration in 1992 parts of the complex, together with additional new buildings, became a hotel, with the main block becoming a casino. Although Eldem was responsible for the restoration, its accuracy must be doubted.

Beşiktaş

ADDRESS 84 Çırağan Caddesi
TRANSPORT bus to Çırağan
ACCESS open (telephone 0212 258 33 77)

Nikoğos and Sarkis Balyan 1874

Beşiktaş

Nikoğos and Sarkis Balyan 1874

Bosphorus bridges

Boğaziçi Köprüsü

The first Bosphorus bridge, which serves as the background for the evening news on Turkish television, is a symbol of modern Istanbul.

The idea of bridging the strait is an ancient one – as far back as 512 BC bridges made up of boats were built across the Bosphorus during wars, the earliest known, for the Persian emperor Darius, at the narrow strait between Rumeli Hisarı and Anadolu Hisarı.

At present two bridges span the Bosphorus. A scheme for a third at the northern end of the strait is highly controversial because its realisation would endanger the already damaged nature reserves.

The first Bosphorus bridge (1970–3), which connects Ortaköy in Beşiktaş with Beylerbeyi in Üsküdar, is 1074 metres long, suspended between two giant piers each 165 metres high that look like gateways to the other continent. The suspension bands carry 60 hollow box sections, each 18 by 33.4 metres and weighing 150 tons. Six lanes of traffic hover 64 metres above the water. The contractors were Freeman Fox & Partners and Petek Company.

The second Bosphorus bridge (1986–8), also designed by British engineer by W C Brown, is of a similar construction but is 10 metres longer (1084 metres free span) with eight lanes of traffic. Like the early Persian bridge it connects Rumeli Hisarı and Anadolu Hisarı and is part of the city's motorway ringroad.

The building of the bridges and of roads along the shores of the Bosphorus has changed the city and the relationship of its inhabitants to the water. Before the construction of the new roads the citizens of Istanbul lived in close contact with the Bosphorus, which was used every day for transportation and fishing. The ferry traffic and leisure activities that grew up around the ferry termini from the mid-nineteenth century onwards made the waterfront a lively urban space. But the 17 cargo ferries

Beşiktas

W C Brown 1970–3/1986–8

Beşiktaş

W C Brown 1970–3/1986–8

crossing the strait almost 650 times a day were unable to cope with demand and waiting times for vehicles were often substantial.

Today only a fraction of travellers cross the Bosphorus by ferry and the quays are underused. Many of the sites along the shores are privately owned and the shore roads form a barrier between the water and the villages behind. The water is no longer the heart of the city but merely a barrier between its shores. However, the construction of the bridges has opened up the Asian side of the city as a vast and accessible living area and broken down the border between the two continents.

It is to be hoped that the planned expansion of the public transport network will help to reactivate the ferry connections and relieve the overcrowded bridges, making the water once more a key urban element.

Beşiktaş

ADDRESS Ortaköy, Beşiktaş to Beylerbeyi, Üsküdar
TRANSPORT bus to Ortaköy or Beylerbeyi
ACCESS open

W C Brown 1970–3/1986–8

Beşiktaş

W C Brown 1970–3/1986–8

The view of the traditional Ortaköy mosque set against the high-tech first Bosphorus bridge (see page 214) is one of the famous sights of Istanbul.

Ortaköy (literally 'middle village') had a population made up of over 40 per cent of non-Muslims during the Ottoman period. Today the rebuilt synagogue (1913), Greek Othodox church of St Phocas (1872) and nine-teenth-century mosque demonstrate the cultural heterogeneity of the Bosphorus village.

The waterfront area around the landing stage has been redesigned by the municipality of Beşiktaş under the direction of Erhan İşözen. New pavements and street lighting have been installed, the landing stage has been refurbished, the *çeşme* (fountain) opposite the mosque has been rebuilt and relocated and the façades of the houses have been restored and painted in collaboration with their owners. The area, now called Ortaköy Square, has become a recreational zone with several trendy shops and restaurants.

The Ortaköy mosque (Mecidiye Camii) occupies a beautiful site, jutting out into the strait. It was built in 1853–5 by Nikoğos Balyan and resembles the Dolmabahçe mosque by Nikoğos' father Garabed. A contemporary of Charles Garnier, Nikoğos studied in Paris and there are similarities between his mosque and Garnier's Paris opera house.

Note the stylistic contrast between the neo-baroque cubic mosque with its single dome and the neo-classical flat porch – as if two autonomous buildings, each in a different architectural language, had been spliced together. The porch building accommodates the two minarets with their stone finials. The mosque itself has corner piers with large turrets framing two-storey tympanums, each with two rows of three large windows.

Inside, the large windows with their tripartite rhythm make the interior space seem light and skeletal, with something of the atmosphere of a

pavilion at sea. The inside melts with the outside through the use of vaulted windows, though the clear glass of the original has been replaced by etched glass to conceal the worshippers at prayer. The walls are richly decorated with real and fake marble. The design deliberately eschews the serious inward-looking atmosphere of earlier mosques.

Also look at the ruins of the Küçük Esna Sultan palace, an early seventeenth-century palace gutted by a fire in 1975, upstream next to the mosque, and the Nadja Sanat Galerisi at 19 Salhane Sokak, a former police station converted into a gallery. To the left of the shore road at the main crossroads is a highly unusual double *hamam* by Sinan, hidden by a modern stucco façade.

Beşiktaş

TRANSPORT bus to Ortaköy; ferry to Ortaköy Vapur İskelesi

Bruno Taut's villa

Bruno Taut's relationship with Turkey goes back to 1916, when he entered an international competition for a 'house of friendship' with a design that was a synthesis of traditional Turkish architecture. In 1936 he was granted political asylum by Atatürk and he lived the last two years of his life in Istanbul, working as an architect, as head of the architecture department of the Turkish Ministry of Education and as a university teacher. He built five schools and took part in several competitions. He was a strong supporter of the regionalist approach championed by the proponents of the second national architectural movement.

Taut had lived in Japan from 1933 and this house demonstrates a mixture of Turkish and Japanese influences. Set in a wooded site on a steep escarpment, the villa fits perfectly into its surroundings. From the outside the double row of windows in the living room and three separate projecting tiled roofs make it look like a three-storey building, but in fact there are only two levels. The octagonal upper floor, glazed on six sides, is crowned by a pyramidal tiled roof which is left exposed on the inside.

The house was designed to have a free view over the Bosphorus, but unfortunately the first Bosphorus bridge destroys the peaceful location.

Taut is the only European buried in the cemetry of Edirne.

Beşiktaş

ADDRESS Muallim Nacı Caddesi, Ortaköy, Beşiktaş
TRANSPORT bus to Ortaköy
ACCESS none

Bruno Taut 1936

Beşiktaş

Bruno Taut 1936

Bosphorus European Side

Fortress of Rumeli
Rumeli Hisarı

The fortress is a museum and a location for open-air concerts and performances. It has a fantastic view over the Bosphorus and is a favourite place for kissing.

The Rumeli fortress was built by Mehmet II in preparation for the siege and conquest of Constantinople. It occupies a site approximately 250 metres long by 120 metres wide on the European side of the strait at its narrowest point (approximately 750 metres wide) opposite the Anadolu fortress on the Asian side built by Beyazit I in 1390–5. Once the Janissaries with their cannon had been installed at Rumeli all shipping could be stopped, preventing supplies of grain from the shores of the Black Sea from reaching Constantinople. Because of its strategic importance to Mehmet's plans, the fortress was built very quickly – some 3000 craftsmen and labourers completed it within four months. After the conquest in 1453 it became redundant; in the sixteenth century the northern tower was used as prison.

The Rumeli fortress is another example of the extraordinary way Ottoman architecture takes advantage of the landscape. With its two round towers (23.8 and 26.7 metres in diameter) on top of the slope and its polygonal tower on the shore, it dominates the entire strait. The fortress has both outer and inner fortifications, the outer one on the east beside the Bosphorus, the inner one on the slope behind. Inside the inner fortification timber houses, a *hamam* and a mosque were built for the 400 people stationed here. The walls, which use stones from nearby ruins, are up to 7 metres thick.

The architects Tekeli, Sisa & Hepgüler (see page 50) won a competition in 1958 to convert the fortress into an open-air museum with a recreational area. They created a central multifunctional space with a freeform amphitheatre and podium in an appropriate landscape. To strengthen the

1451–2

sculptural effect of the walls, later additions were demolished and new interventions subtly integrated: facilities such as offices and kitchens have been sited under modest platforms; new retaining walls are inconspicuous; footpaths and terraces with panoramic views have been created. Simple green landscaping supplies an unobtrusive background that emphasises Rumeli's dynamic architecture.

The Anadolu fortress – a square main tower surrounded by an inner wall with four towers and an outer wall with three towers – is very picturesque, with the old houses and mansions of the village of Anadolu clustered around it, but there is no access to it.

ADDRESS Rumeli Hisarı Caddesi, behind Bebek
TRANSPORT bus 22, 25E to Rumeli Hisarı
ACCESS open 9.30–17.00 except Mondays

Bosphorus European side

1451–2

Şemsettin Sirer mansion
Şemsettin Sirer Yalısı

Both the street and waterfront façades of this modernist mansion retain the character and scale of the traditional *yalı* (see page 234). Eldem's characteristic use of vertical façade elements (compare the Social Security Agency complex, page 42), combined with the double balconies and wide terraces overlooking the Bosphorus on each floor, demonstrates a convincing integration of modernism and local architectural tradition.

But the plan of the four-storey house eschews that of the traditional *yalı*. The narrowness of the site is compensated for by the depth of the building, with services and bathrooms placed against the blind wall. The entrance level has a hall opening on to a terrace at the water's edge; the first floor contains the kitchen, living and dining rooms; the second floor houses the bedrooms with a traditional bay window overlooking the street. Finally – an Eldem trademark – a sauna and sundeck are hidden behind the wide roof with its overhanging eaves.

Yeniköy has several noteworthy art noveau buildings, especially the Şehzade Burhanettin Yalısı.

ADDRESS 163 Köybaşı Caddesi, Yeniköy
TRANSPORT bus 41D, 42 to Yeniköy or by boat from Eminönü İskelesi
ACCESS none

Sedad Hakkı Eldem 1966–7

Bosphorus European side

Sedad Hakkı Eldem 1966–7

Büyükdere house

The large village of Büyükdere was where the Russian, British, Danish, Swedish, Austrian and other embassies built their summer residences in the eighteenth century – a place from which to enjoy the nearby Black Sea and to walk in the Belgrad forest with its aqueducts and reservoirs.

The two houses at the end of Kahkaha Çiçeği Sokağı were built in the nineteenth century and renovated in 1992–4. The main house has a concrete frame with timber cladding in the traditional red-brown colour, traditional overhanging eaves, a bay window with a balcony supported on brackets and vertical windows with shutters that give the façade two different aspects depending on whether they are open or closed. A third-floor extension added at the beginning of this century destroyed the harmony of the proportions. The renovation restored the house to its original form.

The façade of the annexe building is rendered in a coarse pink-red plaster. The contrasts of façade materials, of the fixed façade of the annexe with the flexible façade of the main house and the hierarchy of the two buildings, emphasised by the topography, make this an intriguing composition.

Also look at the three terraced houses at 6 Çobankızı Sokağı.

ADDRESS Kahkaha Çiçeği Sokağı, Büyükdere
TRANSPORT bus 41, 41D, 41M to Büyükdere
ACCESS none

Mehmet Karaören, İhsan Bilgin, Fatoş Karaören, Süha Kizildere

Sariyer mansions
Sariyer Yalısı

Sariyer is the largest village on the European shore of the Bosphorus and the site of many *yalı*s, the waterside summer residences of the Ottoman aristocracy.

Sited along the banks of the Bosphorus with a backdrop of wooded hills, the *yalı*s – built mostly from the seventeenth to nineteenth centuries – form part of Istanbul's image and identity. These timber mansions have a similar architectural relationship to the water as Venetian palaces, and Istanbul is sometimes known as the 'wooden Venice'. Mansions for the Turkish princes were concentrated on the lower Bosphorus, those of Greeks and Armenians at Kuruçeşme and the *yalı*s of European ambassadors at Tarabya and Büyükdere.

The variety of form of the *yalı*s owes much to their freedom from the planning restrictions in operation in the inner city. Traditionally sited on the waterfront, typical elements include balconies projecting over the water (*cumba*s), overhanging eaves, and projecting bays, often of daring form and construction. Terracotta-coloured timber (a tone known as 'Ottoman pink') and tiled roofs are also characteristic.

In plan, the *yalı*s were based around a central space, the *sofa*, usually square or oval, which was used as the main living space and from which the other rooms were reached. A *yalı* would usually have two main entrances on opposite sides of the *sofa*, one from the waterfront and one from the garden. The entrances opened on to antechambers which were typically separated from the *sofa* by a pair of columns and a low balustrade. The *sofa*, the two antechambers and the two main entrances would lie on the main axis of the house. Sometimes a cross-axis would be formed by two more antechambers, creating a cruciform *sofa*. The secondary rooms (bedrooms) would fill in the corners of the cruciform, and the antechambers on the cross-axis would have further entrances or staircases

leading to the floor above. In some *yalı*s the *sofa* and its antechambers would be a single continuous space.

In larger *yalı*s the *sofa* would have a domed roof in reference to nomads' tents. Rows of windows overlooked the garden and water; one of these would be a double row, the upper set glazed with coloured glass, the lower one at the eye level of a seated person. Retractable slatted timber grilles, divided horizontally, facilitated the regulation of climate and light and in the *harem* obscured views of the women within, who were not allowed to be seen in public without a veil, while allowing views out. Buffered from the external heat by the auxiliary rooms, and with a central marble fountain and 'musical' fountains (*şelsebil*s) set into its walls, the *sofa* was one of the coolest spaces in the house. It would usually be sparsely furnished, with a low lounging divan (*sedir*) at one end, though other items of furniture were introduced in the early nineteenth century. Sometimes the water side would have bays with windows on three sides projecting out over the water supported on wooden brackets.

Rooms for men and women were strictly separated until the beginning of the twentieth century, with the men occupying the *selamlık* and the women the *harem*. Originally the *harem* and *selamlık* occupied different buildings with a courtyard or garden in between, each arranged according to the plan described above. Many of the larger *yalı*s had their own *hamam*s, usually also in a separate building.

Most *yalı*s had imposing staircases and grand, spacious rooms. Carpets and bedding were stored in wall cupboards during the day and other items such as porcelain in chests. During the eighteenth century the rooms would be decorated with rococo details, though the straightforward floor plans and simple outward appearance of the *yalı*s remained unchanged.

At the beginning of the nineteenth century the flamboyant and ornate

baroque style was replaced by the cooler, more restrained empire style (1808–67), which in turn was superseded by the eclectic cosmopolitian style (1867–1908). In the second half of the nineteenth century *yalıs* began to be set back from the Bosphorus rather than sited on the waterfront. In addition to the traditional red-brown treatment of the façade, pastel colours such as cream, pink and lemon were introduced. Between 1905 and 1914, under the influence of Raimondo D'Aronco (see page 132), several *yalıs* were built in an art nouveau style.

Most of the surviving *yalıs* are in the empire or cosmoplitan styles. They are characterised by orthogonal floor plans, louvres and mesh screens rather than grilles and doors opening on to the water. The reasons for the lack of older surviving *yalıs* include land speculation, the ephemerality of timber structures, constantly at risk from domestic fires, the tradition whereby land returned to the sultan after the death of its occupant rather than being passed down to the family, and the Islamic stricture that secular buildings be temporary in nature.

See also the Fethi Paşa Yalısı and Mocan Yalısı at Kuzguncuk; Hekimbaşı Yalısı and Count Ostrorog Yalısı at Kandilli; Kibrisli Mustafa Emin Paşa Yalısı at Küçüksu (1760); Koç Yalısı at Anadolu Hisarı (1911); Sarfet Paşa Yalısı (1750) and Kanlıca Huber Yalısı at Tarabya; Sait-Halim-Paşa-Yalısı (1860) and Afif-Paşa-Yalısı at Yeniköy; and Şerifler-Yalısı (1782) at Emirgân.

TRANSPORT boat from Eminönü İskelesi

Bosphorus Asian Side

Eczacı Ethem Pertev Yalısı

Eczacı Ethem Pertev Yalısı – a two-storey timber building with a red clay tiled roof – is in the cosmopolitian style (1867–1908, see Bosphorus mansions, page 234). Though the way it projects over the water is traditional, the artistically carved balconies, brackets and gable boards are typical of the nineteenth century. The ground floor is set back to form a veranda. The façade is dominated by high, vertically proportioned sash windows with low sills, some still with traditional shutters, and decorative carved wood. A frieze between the two storeys runs around the entire building.

ADDRESS Kanlıca
TRANSPORT bus 15F to Kanlıca or boat from Eminönü İskelesi
ACCESS none

late nineteenth century

Bosphorus Asian side

late nineteenth century

Köprülü mansion
Köprülü Yalısı

The Köprülü Yalısı was the residence of the Grand Vezir Amcazade Hüseyin Paşa and was the scene of the signing of the Peace of Carlowitz between Turkey and the European powers in 1699. Built in the classical Ottoman style, it is now in poor condition. It has lost its two-storey *harem*, with its coloured-glass windows and overhanging eaves, and only the *selamlık* survives.

The cruciform plan was a traditional element in Ottoman house architecture until the nineteenth century (see page 234). Here, as in many of the larger *yalı*s, the central *sofa* or hall with its marble fountain is surmounted by a wooden dome and opens on to three bays that project over the water supported on wooden brackets. Within the bays were placed the divans or *sedir*s from which one enjoyed a panoramic view of the Bosphorus. A series of panels above the windows, where usually another row of windows would be placed, was painted with floral motifs and acted as a kind of 'case' for the sliding windows, which would disappear when they were pulled up. The most impressive aspect of the interior is the painted decor.

ADDRESS between Kanlıca and Anadolu Hisarı
TRANSPORT boat from Eminönü İskelesi
ACCESS none

Palace of Küçüksu

Küçüksu Kasrı

The design for the Palace of Küçüksu was modelled on Nikoğos Balyan's earlier Ihlamur pavilion at Teşvikiye, which elaborated the formal language of the Dolmabahçe palace gates (see page 194). The idea of two flanking terraces supported on sculptural stone columns was realised at Ihlamur and later repeated at Küçüksu.

Replacing a previous timber construction, the royal summer residence, built for Abdül Mecit I, is sited between two streams on a beautiful meadow by the Bosphorus known as the 'Sweet Waters of Asia' – a favourite resort of the Ottoman elite and still popular today. Its baroque façades notwithstanding, the palace pays respect to its Ottoman heritage by employing the dimensions and proportions of the traditional *yalı*.

The sultan and his followers would arrive by boat, so a lot of effort was expended on the waterfront entrance. The richly decorated gate opens on to a double staircase built around a fountain; on the upper level a portico with eclectic columns gives entry to the symmetrically arranged building. The façade is sculpted with reliefs and pilasters, though it is said that the sultan claimed this richly decorated building was too sober.

Inside, each of the two storeys has four corner rooms and a central hall or *sofa*, a traditional cruciform plan reminiscent of that of the Çinili Köşkü (see Topkapı palace, page 92). The building is currently being restored.

ADDRESS Küçüksu Caddesi, between Kandilli and Anadolu Hisarı
TRANSPORT bus 15H to Küçüksu
ACCESS (after restoration) daily 9.30–16.00, except Mondays and Thursdays

Bosphorus Asian side

Nikoğos Balyan 1856

Nikoğos Balyan 1856

Suna Kiraç mansion
Suna Kiraç Yalısı

The Suna Kiraç mansion is one of several *yalıs* built by Eldem for Turkey's rich industrialists and businessmen. In the course of his career (see Social Security Agency complex, page 42), Eldem carried out much research into the buildings along the Bosphorus and as a member of the Supreme Council of Historic Sites and Monuments – the institution that approves the demolition or restoration of all historic buildings – he had a big influence on the face of the waterfront.

The simplicity of form and materials in the Suna Kiraç mansion exemplifies Eldem's rational interpretation of traditional architecture. The highly transparent, vertically proportioned façade, made up of glazed rectangles and red-brown louvres framed by white borders, has historical origins and is at the same time an Eldem trademark. The tiled roofs with overhanging eaves, lemon stucco panels and position of the mansion – set back from the water behind a narrow quay – are typical of *yalıs* of the second half of the nineteenth century.

Inside, the central *sofa* is double height, flanked by living areas on the ground floor and bedrooms on the upper level.

ADDRESS Vaniköy
TRANSPORT boat from Eminönü İskelesi
ACCESS none

Sedad Hakkı Eldem 1965–6

Sedad Hakkı Eldem 1965–6

Sadullah Paşa mansion
Sadullah Paşa Yalısı

The *harem* of the Sadullah Paşa mansion – the only part still in existence – cannot be dated precisely, though during the restoration of 1949 by architect Turgut Cansever structural and ornamental elements characteristic of the sixteenth and seventeenth centuries were found. Other sources claim the mansion was built for a grand vezir of Mustafa III in 1760.

The symmetrical terracotta-coloured timber façade with its bays projecting over the water supported on brackets, vertical window treatment and grilles are typical features of the *yalı* (see page 234). Behind the dignified façade there is a graceful interior with baroque decoration combined with Ottoman elements. The ground floor has an octagonal *sofa* with entrances on four sides and antechambers on the water and garden sides. The door to the waterfront is a step lower than the others to facilitate arrival by boat. The upper level has an oval *sofa* with a sitting recess which opens on to the view over the Bosphorus, a baroque fountain, murals of landscapes and a painted dome. Adjoining the *sofa* are four bedrooms with small ancillary rooms with views of the garden or the water.

Originally the door on the north façade opened on to the *selamlık* and to the north-east were additional kitchen and storage facilities with a high ceiling. At present the building is again under restoration, this time by Turgut Cansever's daughter Feyza, and the north façade has been altered to match the southern one.

Also look at the Kuleli Askeri Lisesi in Kuleli/Çengelköy.

ADDRESS Çengelköy
TRANSPORT boat from Eminönü İskelesi
ACCESS none

restoration Turgut and Feyza Cansever 1949 and 1996

restoration Turgut and Feyza Cansever 1949 and 1996

Üsküdar and Kadıköy

Shell general headquarters
Shell Genel Müdürlüğü

The polychrome façade makes reference neither to J P Kleihues' Frankfurt Museum für Vor- und Frühgeschichte nor to James Stirling's Stuttgart Nationalgalerie. It is Shell's red and yellow logo that inspired the alternating stripes of natural red and yellow sandstone.

The complex inflates the cruciform plan of the traditional Ottoman house (see Sariyer mansions, page 234) to an urban scale by placing four blocks around a central circulation space (the equivalent of a *sofa*). In addition, the two circulation axes are terminated by buildings: one a semicylindrical structure housing a café and auditorium, the other a restored pre-existing building that serves as an annexe to one of the blocks. As well as ensuring that the office spaces have similar qualities in terms of light and views, the arrangement bypasses local building restrictions that prohibit façades longer than 30 metres. A successful play of inside and outside and positive and negative space is achieved.

The horizontally striped façades are repeated on all the buildings to give the complex unity. The elevations combine post-modern elements with the geometric language of modernism. The blocks are constructed from insitu concrete frames with sandstone curtain walls; the base of the old building is in quarrystone; and the small building is in fairfaced concrete. Though the standard of construction is high, the use of too many different materials and elements detracts from the stringency of the whole.

The complex provides 11,000 square metres of floorspace for 250 staff on a 16,000-square-metre site. The winning entry to a limited competition organised by Shell, it took 17 months to build following a seven-month design period. Attentive research into sources of materials made it relatively inexpensive.

To satisfy the client's need for security, the complex is located as far

Nevzat Sayın & Gökhan Avcıoğlu 1990

as possible from the street entrance. The guarded parking area is at the entrance to the site, with a garden area between the parking and the building complex.

Nevzat Sayın was also the architect for the Gön leather factory (see page 276).

ADDRESS Oymacı Sokak/Kuşbakışı Caddesi, Bağlarbaşı, Altunizade, Üsküdar
TRANSPORT bus 14K, 14T, 14Y to Altunizade
ACCESS by appointment (telephone 0216 391 57 00)

Nevzat Sayın & Gökhan Avcıoğlu 1990

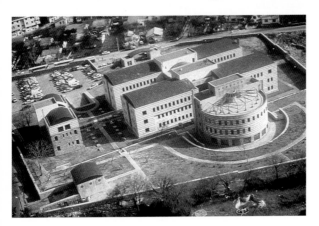

Üsküdar and Kadıköy

Nevzat Sayın & Gökhan Avcıoğlu 1990

Hasol mansion

Hasol Yalısı

Two architects, a husband (editor of Turkish architecture magazine *yapı*) and wife, bought this old waterfront mansion and converted it into their own residence.

The original structure was a massive brick building situated in a 350-square-metre garden between the coast road and the water. Built in the 1930s, it had no specific architectural or historic value and so was not registered by the Bosphorus Conservation Committee, allowing the architects the freedom to remodel it as they wished.

The factor which interested them most was the location, with its panoramic view of Stamboul and the Bosphorus shore as far as the first Bosphorus bridge, and this became the focal point of the design. So as not to compete with the splendid surroundings, they decided to keep the architecture as simple as possible, retaining the outer massive walls with the exception of the waterfront façade, which was replaced by a glazed wall with a double-height bay to maximise the view. Inside, the massive structure was eliminated and replaced by steel elements.

The three-storey main building, connected to the road by a wood-and-steel bridge, contains the living area and bedrooms. Between the road and the main house is an annexe used as a guest house and caretaker's lodge. A paved platform at the waterfront and a terrace garden with the original fruit and palm trees create an intimate relationship between inside and outside.

ADDRESS 61 Paşalimanı Caddesi, Üsküdar
CIVIL ENGINEER Necmi Üstüner
TRANSPORT ferry to Üsküdar İskelesi
ACCESS none

A Hayzuran Hasol, Doğan Hasol, Has Mimalık Project Group 1993–4

Şemsi Ahmet Paşa mosque
Şemsi Ahmet Paşa Camii

During the Ottoman period Üsküdar was a popular location for mosques, perhaps because of a belief that the Asian side of the city was closer to the home of the prophet. Many mosques were built by valide sultans and eminent citizens and every year there was a big caravan from Üsküdar to Mecca and Medina financed by the sultan. Until the 1970s, its many mosques and timber mansions gave Üsküdar a charmingly oriental character but today it is a bustling satellite town of Istanbul.

The Şemsi Ahmet Paşa mosque is one of Sinan's most beautiful late works. The client, Beylerbey of Anatolia, was a poet and philosopher from the Ottoman nobility who for some months acted as grand vezir to Süleyman. His foundation is comparatively modest.

The complex lies directly on the Bosphorus waterfront. A door set in a wall with grilled windows leads from the quay into the irregularly shaped courtyard which is surrounded on two sides by the L-shaped *medrese* with its arcades and domed *dershane* (lecture hall). On the narrowest side of the courtyard opposite the quay is the entrance to the small mosque.

The interior could not be more simple: an 8-metre cube that becomes an octogan in plan where it supports the dome. Rather than the usual freestanding *türbe*, here the founder's mausoleum opens on to the mosque, separated only by a grille.

Also look at Sinan's İskele mosque (1547) near Üsküdar İskelesi and the nearby Karaça Ahmet cemetery.

ADDRESS Şemsi Paşa Caddesi, Üsküdar
TRANSPORT ferry to Üsküdar İskelesi
ACCESS open

Sinan 1580

Çürüksulu Ahmet Paşa mansion

Çürüksulu Ahmet Paşa Yalısı

Sited on top of a hill, the Çürüksulu Ahmet Paşa mansion, named after an Ottoman general, looks out over Stamboul with views of the Topkapı palace, Hagia Sophia and the Sultan Ahmet mosque. Originally on the banks of the Sea of Marmara, today it is separated from the water by a road. The red-brown façade with its vertically proportioned windows and timber louvres is surrounded by greenery.

The building was restored for the diplomat Nuri Birgi. The timber frame, roof and façade were reconstructed, heating, plumbing and wiring systems replaced and the building repainted – a low-budget job intended to demonstrate the possibilities for similar historic houses. In the course of the restoration decoration probably dating from the sixteenth, eighteenth and nineteenth centuries was uncovered.

Also look at Leander's tower (Kız Kulesi) on an islet 200 metres off the coast of Salacak.

ADDRESS 11 Muhtar Şahin Sokağı, Salacak, Üsküdar
TRANSPORT ferry to Üsküdar İskelesi
ACCESS none

Üsküdar and Kadıköy

restoration Turgut Cansever 1968–71

restoration Turgut Cansever 1968–71

Haydarpaşa station
Haydarpaşa İstasyonu

Although the Haydarpaşa–İzmit railway dates from 1873, the station, a gift from Kaiser Wilhelm of Germany as part of his attempt to engage the sultan in economic and military collaboration, was not built until 1909.

The station is the most important terminus of the Anatolian railway system and the end stop for trains from as far away as Bagdad. There is still no rail connection between Istanbul's European and Asian shores so travellers wishing to continue their journey must cross the Bosphorus by ferry, though a railway from Sirkeci to Üsküdar, with a connection to Söğütlüçeşme on the Anatolian line, is under consideration.

The imposing neo-classical terminus resembles a German castle. With its mixture of styles and motifs, it is a good example of eclectic architecture. The predominantly neo-classical façade is divided horizontally into three sections with the attic enlivened by Dutch gables and a corner tower with a gothic conical roof. Sirkeci, the oriental-looking station on the European side, and Haydarpaşa, the western-style station on the Asian side, are good examples of the combination of influences that has shaped Istanbul.

Also look at the Haydarpaşa İskelesi next to the station and the Haydarpaşa Lisesi (university).

ADDRESS Haydapaşa İstasyon Caddesi, Haydarpaşa, Kadıköy
TRANSPORT ferry to Haydarpaşa İskelesi
ACCESS open

Otto Ritter & Helmuth Cuno 1909

Otto Ritter & Helmuth Cuno 1909

Outskirts

Atatürk's summer residence
Atatürk Deniz Köşkü

After an apprenticeship with Vedat Tek (see page 112), Seyfettin Nasih Arkan (1902–66) worked in Germany for five years with Hans Poelzig. Following his modernist winning entry to the competition for the Minister of Foreign Affairs' residence in the new capital of Ankara (1933–4), he was asked by Atatürk to design the presidential summer residence in Florya.

The unpretentious white stuccoed, Bauhaus-influenced building stands on piles in the Sea of Marmara and is connected to the beach by a 90-metre footbridge. It is divided into two parts: a 46 by 9-metre rectangle containing the services, set at right angles to the beach, and a 50 by 11.25-metre section running parallel to the beach and surrounded by terraces. This housed Atatürk's private and state rooms and a guest area with a view towards the sea.

Atatürk used the residence for political conferences and to entertain foreign guests, a tradition continued by subsequent presidents. In 1988 the building was handed over for restoration to the Department for National Palaces and it is now the Atatürk museum.

ADDRESS Florya, telephone 0212 579 06 20
TRANSPORT train from Sirkeci to Florya, then bus; or bus 98F to Florya
ACCESS 1 October–28 February 9.30–16.00; 1 March–30 September 9.30–17.00; closed Monday and Thursday

Seyfettin Nasih Arkan 1935

Seyfettin Nasih Arkan 1935

Uğur private college
Özel Uğur Koleji

This addition to an existing private school is situated on an empty plot beside the E5 highway.

The complex is planned to contain two six-storey rectangular buildings accommodating a primary and a secondary school (phase two) with a cylindrical administration building. These buildings enclose a yard, with the two schools built on pilotis to increase the available space.

All shared facilities – the auditorium, sports hall, gym and a swimming pool used by the public in the evening – are located in the basement. The auditorium is blue-painted reinforced concrete with blue fittings. The entrance, which will eventually be in the secondary school, is at present a temporary tent. The two upper levels of the primary school house a nursery school and canteen.

The organisation of the primary school is clear and simple. The staircase runs parallel to the façade to protect the classrooms facing the courtyard from the sun. The full-height windows above the doors between the classrooms and the corridor and the ubiquitous use of primary colours produce interesting views and a light and friendly atmosphere.

Unfortunately the architects were not asked to supervise the school's construction and too wide a variety of materials has been used. The short construction time (eight months) and low budget do not excuse the shabby details, especially the brickwork of the façades.

ADDRESS Florya Beşyol Sanayı Merkezi, telephone 0212 592 17 31
STRUCTURAL ENGINEER İsmail Akyıldız
CONTRACTOR Alihan Haydaroğlu
TRANSPORT bus 76B to Beşyol
ACCESS ask at reception during term time

Kerem Erginoğlu & Hasan Çalışlar 1995

Kerem Erginoğlu & Hasan Çalışlar 1995

Sabah newspaper works

Sabah Gazete baskı ve İşletme Tesisi

Because of the density of the inner city of Istanbul, this major newspaper decided to locate its new building in İkitelli, an industrial zone on the outskirts, where future expansion would be possible.

The shape of the site suggested a long rectangular building, 108 metres by 36 metres, its four storeys and basement designed to allow for flexibility and change. The offices are mostly open plan, flanked by atriums which create interesting views. The building uses the most up-to-date technology and makes a feature of the drama of the massive printing presses and the advanced communication technologies within.

The east and west sides consist of three towers, each 9 metres square, containing services and vertical circulation, between which are atriums with glazed roofs. If there is a fire the atriums function like chimneys: skylights open automatically to draw out the smoke.

The 60 by 60-centimetre plan module was selected to conform with the coffered slabs that support the raised tile floors. The 50-centimetre space between the slab and the floor houses the services for both the ceiling (ambience lighting, smoke detectors, communication systems, air exhaust outlets, etc.) and the floor (air conditioning outlets, wiring, etc.), all arranged in modular trays. The free circulation of heated or cooled air in this space proved an economical and flexible solution to temperature regulation, since the outlet grilles can be rearranged to conform with any office configuration. This, and the cheap construction materials, allowed the cost to be kept down to US$500 per square metre, including good furniture.

The exterior has an aluminium frame with silicon gaskets supporting anti-solar double glazing and the interior aluminium frames support laminated glass with EPDM lining. The main roof consists of sound-absorbing, perforated aluminium sandwich panels supported on a stru-

Mehmet Konuralp 1988–90

Outskirts

Mehmet Konuralp 1988–90

tural space frame. Unfortunately the exterior does not do justice to the disciplined organisation and sensitive design of the interior and the careful detailing – by Turkish standards.

In addition to the editorial, design, advertising and administrative offices for various magazines and newspapers and the press hall, the building also contains recreational and social facilities to compensate for its distant location from the city centre. Between 2500 and 3000 people work there and an extension by another architect, unfortunately in a very different style, has just been started.

ADDRESS Sabah Tesisleri, İkitelli
CONSULTANT ARCHITECT Alpaslan Ataman
STRUCTURAL ENGINEERS Prof. Hasan Karataş; Dilek Cebeci
CONTRACTOR Konrualp Müt. Müs. AŞ
TRANSPORT bus 89C, 98
ACCESS by appointment (telephone 0212 550 49 00)

Outskirts

Mehmet Konuralp 1988–90

Mehmet Konuralp 1988–90

Gön leather factory
Gön Deri Ürünleri Fabrikası

The Gön leather factory stands in stark contrast with its mediocre surroundings and soon became a landmark in an area that has grown up with no regard for urban planning.

The building, on a 10,000-square-metre site, was constructed in two phases. Phase one comprises a 3200-square-metre factory building connected at first-floor level by a glazed bridge to an administration block of similar size. The four-storey factory has workshops on each floor – an unusual arrangement for an industrial building, but one which suits the demands of the manufacturing process, since the departments can easily be moved around to cope with variations in the work flow and the requirements of different products. The three-storey administration block contains the entrance, reception and displays of traditional leather craft on the ground floor, with more showrooms on the first floor and offices on the top floor.

Because all the details were designed to make the production process as simple as possible and inexpensive materials were used for construction, the building was no more expensive than any other of similar type. In addition, the architect acted as contractor, which resulted in considerable savings.

The phase-two building, connected via a bridge to the factory, is more consistent in its architecture, using a more restricted range of materials: glass, steel, precast concrete and aluminium window frames. The three floors open on to a triple-height atrium. The huge windows and glass roof above the entrance hall and the elliptical void make it a light place to work. The pleasant top-floor canteen has a barrel-vaulted concrete roof clad in copper, with porthole windows in one wall and extensive windows and glass doors opening on to a roof garden in the other.

As well as being an attractive design, the complex has been constructed

Nevzat Sayın 1988–91, 1995

Nevzat Sayın 1988–91, 1995

to incorporate many practical ideas, such as the collection and recycling of rain water.

Phase two, which won the Turkish architecture award in 1996, is an extremely convincing piece of modern architecture inside and out that is well worth the journey outside Istanbul.

ADDRESS 159 Küçükköy Cebeci Caddesi, Gaziosmanpaşa
CONTRACTOR Nevzat Sayın/Hasan Elmas (Gön)
TRANSPORT bus 88A then taxi
ACCESS by appointment (telephone 0212 538 48 50)

Outskirts

Nevzat Sayın 1988–91, 1995

Nevzat Sayın 1988–91, 1995

Vefateks Fabrikası mosque
Vefateks Fabrikası Camii

There has been little attempt to translate the mosque into modern architectural language: two examples exist, one on Heybeli Island, the other in Yeniköy. The privately financed Vefateks Fabrikası mosque, at present only a project, takes a minimalist approach, reducing the form to the basics of space and function.

An Anatolian mosque traditionally consists of a square domed room with a *mihrab* (prayer niche) in its south-east wall facing Mecca, a gallery or side room for women, at least one minaret and an outdoor court or indoor vestibule. Here Nevzat Sayın has dispensed with the dome and the minaret (redundant because chants are no longer sung from towers but blasted out from prerecorded tapes through loudspeakers). The traditional cubic space of the Anatolian mosque is combined with the long *mihrab* wall typical of an Arabic mosque. This penetrates a glazed opening to continue outside, allowing worshippers inside and outside to pray in a single row. The lack of distinction between inside and outside is further accentuated by continuous paving. The women's section is positioned along the back wall of the main space, allowing them to look directly at the *mihrab*.

The low-budget building will be constructed of fairfaced concrete, with the *mihrab* wall painted turquoise and an abstraction of the word 'Allah' etched into the north-west wall. Otherwise glass, stone and timber will be used.

A very interesting building is expected – completion is anticipated to be by the end of 1997.

ADDRESS 163 Küçükköy Cebeci Caddesi, Gaziosmanpaşa
CLIENT Yusuf Bolluk
TRANSPORT bus 88A, then taxi

Nevzat Sayın 1997–

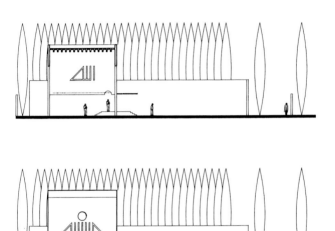

Nevzat Sayın 1997–

Tercüman offices

The Tercüman newspaper building was designed at a time when Turkish architecture was seaching for a new formal vocabulary and vulnerable to the influence of international trends – a time when pluralism took command. A contemporary of Kisho Kurokawa's Nakagin Capsule Tower (1972), the building resembles a flat airport tower overlooking the speeding cars of the E5 highway.

Architectural historian Bülent Özer has described the building as a 'successful contemporary interpretation of the classical language'. Each of the façades at upper-floor level is made up of three projecting square units flanked by horizontal windows: a large-scale, modern version of the traditional bay. The flat roof is defined by the small towers of the service cores, which add to the overall sculptural effect and reduce the horizontality of the building. The lower levels are less rigid in plan and adapt to the constraints of the surroundings.

At first the building was used by the Tercüman company but it is alleged that the structure was unable to support the heavy printing presses. It was subsequently used as a school for eight years and is now a plastics depot for the Sabancı holding company and in poor condition.

The same architects also designed the Istanbul Reklam building (see page 102).

page 102

ADDRESS Mevlevihane Yolu/Gümüşsuyu Davutpaşa Caddesi, parallel to E5, Merkez Efendi
TRANSPORT tram (direction Zeytinburnu) to A O Yurdu
ACCESS none

Outskirts

Çilingiroğlu & Tunca 1974

Çilingiroğlu & Tunca 1974

Mağlova aqueduct
Mağlova Kemer

Romantically hidden in dense forest, difficult to find but worth the search.

The hilly terrain of Istanbul's outskirts made a totally underground water-supply system impractical. The system is an expression of continuity from Byzantine to Ottoman times, with the legacies of each period interwoven.

The Ottoman water system, like other major constructions, was a pious foundation since it was perceived as being for the public good. The Kırkçeşme (40 fountains) artery, one of the four main arteries serving the city, was built under Süleyman to convey water to the lower parts of Stamboul. It was reputedly the longest at the time – at the end of the eighteenth century it was capable of transporting 12,600 cubic metres of water per day – and is also the richest architecturally. The artery has four aqueducts by Sinan, of which the Mağlova is the most impressive.

The structure spanning the valley consists of two storeys of four wide arches framed by three levels of narrow arches. (Sinan used a similar rhythm for the court of his Süleymaniye mosque, see page 64). The five bridge piers are supported by buttresses. The aqueduct is 265 metres long and 35 metres high, but the massive stone construction appears skeletal and light, like gothic tracery.

Also worth seeing are the three other aqueducts of the Kırkçeşme artery: Uzun Kemer (716 metres), Güzelce Kemer and Eğri Kemer.

ADDRESS Alibey Deresi, between Alibeyköy and Kemerburgaz, near Cebeciköy
TRANSPORT bus 99, 47 to Alibeyköy, then *dolmuş* to Kemerburgaz, then taxi

Sinan 1563

Sinan 1563

Holy district of Eyüp

Although much of the area around the Golden Horn has been spoiled by industrialisation, the village of Eyüp – site of one of the most sacred of Muslim shrines and a place of pilgrimage for Muslims from around the world – is still worth visiting because of its atmosphere, especially on Fridays when the areas around the tombs and mosques are so crowded with people at prayer that there is barely room to walk.

According to legend, the grave of Abu Eyüp al Ansari – a companion of the prophet Muhammed who died in the first Arab siege of Constantinople in 674–8 – was miraculously discovered during the Ottoman siege of 1453. A *türbe* and mosque were built on its site by Mehmet II, probably around 1458, together with a *medrese*, *han*, *hamam*, bazaar and *imaret*. The complex was extended in 1591 under Murat III and after falling into disrepair following an earthquake was demolished in 1798 and rebuilt two years later under Selim III.

The mosque, with its large central dome combined with eight half domes, is a baroque copy of Sinan's Azap Kapı mosque (1577–8) in Galata. The court was the scene of a ceremony similiar to the coronation of western monarchs in which new Ottoman sultans were girded with the sword of Osman, founder of the Ottoman (Osmanli) dynasty. Opposite the mosque's entrance is Abu Eyüp al Ansari's tomb, clad with tiles from many periods. The interior is also clad in tiles and the sarcophagus is surrounded by a baroque silver screen.

The large cemetery on the hill above the mosque contains the splendid tombs of some 30 dignitaries, including one sultan. The older tombstones are sculpted with symbols that indicate the profession, sex and age of their owners: turbans signify men, flowers and mussels women. Graves consist of two upright gravestones, the higher one bearing the symbols.

To the south of the cemetery on Defterdar Caddesi is the Zal Mahmut

Paşa mosque, built around 1575 by Sinan. Its *külliye* comprises two *medrese*s and a *türbe* on different levels connected by a staircase. The exterior of the mosque, with its square polychromatic façade, looks more like a palace. Inside a single large dome roofs a space which is impressive in its simplicity.

ADDRESS Eyüp Sultan Camii in Cami-i-Kebir Sokağı, Eyüp
TRANSPORT bus 99 or 99A to Eyüp
ACCESS open

Princes' Isles

Introduction

The Princes' Isles are a group of nine islands off the Asian coast of the Sea of Marmara some 15 to 30 kilometres south of Istanbul. The four largest are Büyükada, Heybeli, Burgaz and Kınalı.

Until the mid-nineteenth century the only buildings on the islands were monasteries, some dating from the seventh century, together with a small number of fishermen's homes on the four larger islands. This changed when a ferry service was established in 1846. Cars were forbidden from 1928 and public transport is provided by horse-drawn carriages.

Büyükada is the biggest and most visited of the islands. The town has several large turn-of-the-century timber villas in a variety of styles. Most are two or three storeys high with elaborate balconies overlooking the sea or woods. The unusual red-brick, neo-gothic house at 55 Çankaya Caddesi was the residence of Leon Trotsky during his exile on Büyükada from 1929 to 1933. The impressive five-storey Hotel Splendid in Nisan Caddesi has corner towers with onion domes.

There are two monasteries on Büyükada. The more interesting is the monastery of St George on the southern hill, a collection of chapels and shrines on three levels with beautiful views in all directions. The monastery of St Nicholas stands on the northern hill.

Buildings to visit on Heybeli include the former Greek Orthodox school of theology on the northernmost hill, rebuilt after the 1894 earthquake, and a tiny Byzantine church with a clover-leaf plan dating from between 1427 and 1439, formerly a monastery chapel and now part of a Turkish naval base, situated to the left of the landing stage (ask permission from the officer in charge).

Burgaz contains some interesting villas. It is worth looking at the Artaç Ev in Metap Sokak, a new house with a cruciform plan by Turgut and Feyza Cansever (the owner may allow access during the summer months).

The landscape of Kınalı is less interesting. It is inhabited and contains several multi-storey buildings with summer apartments.

The five remaining islands are inhabited only during the summer months. Sedef, which has some elegant villas, and Tavşan, which is uninhabited, can be accessed by boats hired on Büyükada. Yassı and the uninhabited Sivri can be seen from Kınalı. Yassı is a military base. For centuries it was a place of imprisonment and exile and among its ruins are those of former monasteries and the nineteenth-century castle of English ambassador Sir Henry Bulwer. The new buildings in front of the castle ruins were used as a prison for former government leaders after the 1960 coup. Kaşik, the smallest of the islands, can be seen from the Heybeli landing stage.

TRANSPORT ferry from Eminönü or Karaköy

Princes' Isles

Anadolu club
Anadolu Kulübü Binası

Designed when the international style was at its height in Turkey, replacing the Ottoman-influenced second national movement with an architecture that is simple, rational and functional, with expressed structure and materials.

The residential Anadolu club, which won first prize in a national competition, combines the international style with ornament – for instance, the finely meshed gold grilles. The street façade, which uses a single repeated element combined with the changing play of open or closed shutters, is similar to recent work by Herzog & de Meuron or Jean Nouvel. The curved concrete roof is influenced by Le Corbusier. The seaward façade, in fairfaced concrete, is made up of a grid of loadbearing cross-walls and projecting slabs which form balconies which at the same time act as *brise-soleils*.

Standing in a neighbourhood of old timber houses, the simplicity of the building makes it an appropriate addition without any attempt at imitating its surroundings.

Princes' Isles

ADDRESS Yirmi Üç Nisan Caddesi, Büyükada
TRANSPORT ferry from Eminönü or Karaköy
ACCESS none

Turgut Cansever & Abdurrahman Hancı 1951

Turgut Cansever & Abdurrahman Hancı 1951

Rıza Derviş villa

With its flat projecting roofs, large glazed areas, reinforced-concrete structure and cantilevered elements, this two-storey house is reminiscent of Frank Lloyd Wright's Falling Water and of the work of Richard Neutra.

The house is L-shaped in plan. The long arm of the L sits on a raised terrace with tremendous views of the sea, with the shorter arm cantilevered out towards the water. The entrance level contains the kitchen, services and main living area with the bedrooms and bathrooms on the upper floor. Both levels are surrounded by terraces and wide balconies with views of the sea and garden. Unfortunately the composition has been damaged slightly by dividing the house into two parts for its brother and sister owners.

The inclusion of timber grilles and other traditional elements demonstrates Eldem's individual interpretation of modernist principles. Eldem also designed the interiors and landscaping, making this a complete architectural statement.

ADDRESS 14 Nizam Caddesi, Büyükada
TRANSPORT ferry from Eminönü or Karaköy
ACCESS none

Sedad Hakkı Eldem 1956–7

Sedad Hakkı Eldem 1956–7

Index

Istanbul: an architectural guide

Istanbul: an architectural guide